Young Writers in the Making

Young Writers in the Making

Sharing the Process with Parents

Alison Preece
and
Diane Cowden

Heinemann
Portsmouth, NH

Heinemann
A division of Reed Publishing (USA) Inc.
361 Hanover Street
Portsmouth, NH 03801-3912

Offices and agents throughout the world

We wish to thank the children and parents who have given their permission to include material in this book. Every effort has been made to contact the copyright holders for permission to reprint borrowed material where necessary. We regret any oversights that may have occurred and would be happy to rectify them in future printings of this work.

Figure 5-3: from *Literacy Begins at Birth* by Marjorie Field (Fisher Books, Tucson, Arizona, 1989). Reprinted by permission.

Library of Congress Cataloging-in-Publication Data

Preece, Alison.
    Young writers in the making : sharing the process with parents /
Alison Preece and Diane Cowden.
      p. cm.
    Includes bibliographical references and index.
    ISBN 0-435-08778-9 (alk. paper)
    1. English language--Composition and exercises--Study and teaching
(Elementary)--Canada. 2. Education, Elementary--Canada--Parent
participation. 3. Home and school--Canada. I. Cowden, Diane.
II. Title.
LB1576.R766   1993
372.6'23'0971--dc20   93-24636
                                                     CIP

Cover "Skunk Story" by Cathy Coates
Cover design by Catherine Hawkes
Printed in the United States of America on acid-free paper
97 96 95 94 93 CP 1 2 3 4 5 6 7

To my mother, Mollie McRae-Thompson
Her encouragement and enthusiasm
throughout my life have inspired me to
fulfill a dream.

Diane

* ◆ *

For *my* parents, Ken and Eve Cavendish . . .
There are none finer.

With much love, Alison

Contents

Contents

Foreword

Norma I. Mickelson, Ph.D.
University of Victoria

There is nothing more important to parents than the education of their children. Therein lies the fulfillment of many of their dreams for their families. For too long parents have been denied partnership in this most significant part of their children's lives—their education!

Alison Preece and Diane Cowden are both parents and professional educators. Together, in Cowden's classroom, they have crafted partnerships in education. In their book *Young Writers in the Making* they outline in detail the co-creation of these partnerships, involving teachers, parents, and children.

Their book is a happy amalgam of theory and practice. They clearly and succinctly answer the question: Why should parents be involved? Further than this, they provide specific guidelines for informing and involving parents in the education of their children. Their answers to commonly asked questions are clear and the actual illustrations of projects that link the home and the school are a delight.

Perhaps one of the greatest strengths of their book is in the section on evaluation. As they note in their final chapter, understanding leads to change.

Preece and Cowden are two of the most creative and successful educators I know. Their book is testament to this fact, providing a blueprint for educational innovation that is long overdue.

Acknowledgments

◆

One of the privileges and perks of being a teacher is the company you keep. This book has been a happy, collaborative undertaking from the outset and there are many friends, family members, colleagues, parents, and children who have had a part in making and shaping it.

Two people warrant a special mention for assistance above and beyond the call of friendship. Bobbi Smith salvaged our book from an over-taxed computer; without her technical expertise, the manuscript might still be in bits and bytes. Daphne Louis' sensitivity to children, and skill with a camera, is evident in many of the photographs that appear on these pages.

We thank and acknowledge all of you: you make all the difference.

To Teachers of Young Writers

◆

This book is for teachers who want to share with parents their knowledge of, and delight in, the writing of young children. After many years of working closely with young children, we are firmly convinced that few things more positively influence the quality of a child's initial school experiences than parents and teachers working together. Over the past decade or so, a great deal has been learned about how young children approach and acquire literacy and, as a result, instructional practices have changed considerably in many classrooms. It's critical that parents be kept abreast of these changes and made aware of the reasons for them. Although excellent books and pamphlets are available to help teachers inform parents about their child's growth as a *reader*, and suggest how they might support that growth, few have much to say about the parental role in supporting a child's beginning efforts as a *writer*. Consequently, this book has been designed to help teachers help parents understand and appreciate the development of children's writing. It is intended as a *practical resource* for the busy teacher. The focus is on meaningful and manageable ways teachers can communicate to parents why they approach writing as they do and how parents can assist their children at home. Our intention is not to present a description of the writing process, nor to provide an overview of writing development; rather, our main goal is to offer support and suggestions to those teachers who are trying to find ways to bring information about both to the parents of the children they teach. To this end the book presents open-ended strategies for informing and involving parents that have been developed and successfully implemented in a variety of settings from preschool through the upper primary years. We hope to confirm the value of reaching out to parents, applaud those teachers who are already doing so, and offer practical encouragement and advice to those who are interested in finding ways to enrich their writing program with parental involvement. When we invite parents to "join us in celebrating and extending what young children do as language learners" (Calkins, 1986, p. 45), everybody gains.

Parents provide caring audiences for young writers.

Why Should Parents Be Involved?

♦

"Writing is learned by writing, by reading, and by perceiving oneself as a writer. . . . Writing is fostered rather than taught. . . What is required is an understanding of what a child faces in learning to write." SMITH, 1982

Parents have many concerns and many questions:

I know teaching has changed from when I went to school, but I honestly don't understand some of the things they are doing nowadays.

Spelling still counts, doesn't it?

Whatever happened to copying from the board?

I realize teachers want to build the children's confidence, but doesn't that come from being shown how to do it right? It seems to me they just let them flounder around, hoping they will figure it out for themselves!

If you don't insist that they learn to write correctly from the beginning aren't you just making it harder for them?

I have been trying to help her with her writing at home, but she keeps saying "my teacher doesn't do it like that."

Questions and comments such as these are especially likely to arise when children are enrolled in classrooms where they are viewed as writers from the very first day of school, where workbooks are disappearing and being replaced with personal journals and child-authored booklets, and where spelling "errors" are recognized as a necessary and acceptable part of learning. Parents often have difficulty appreciating the rationale behind some of the instructional approaches currently being implemented (for example, haven't we all been faced with the doubled-edged enquiry: "Wouldn't he learn more if his work was corrected?"). Confusion is understandable if the instruction their child is experiencing differs dramatically from what they themselves received at school. Misunderstandings easily arise and can quickly translate into concern and anxiety. If such misunderstandings are to be satisfactorily resolved, however, more than the provision of information is required. As Gunderson and Shapiro (1988) observed, "Parents must understand the rationale behind the approach. Otherwise, they tend to react negatively to papers with invented spellings and no apparent 'teacher corrections'" (p. 435). Teachers are increasingly faced with the additional tasks of reassuring and involving parents. As well as helping parents gain insight into the paths and patterns of writing development, teachers also need to demonstrate to them, in ways that convince and calm fears, that our goal, like theirs, is to ensure that their children become competent writers and conventional spellers.

The desirability of close communication between home and school, where informed parents can work with teachers to reinforce and extend the school program, is increasingly being recognized (Clark, Lotto, & MacCarthy, 1980; Epstein, 1988; Fullan, 1991). Research provides clear evidence that parents want to be involved (Epstein, 1986), and that such involvement results in positive outcomes with respect to student learning and student and parent attitudes. Many teachers want to involve parents in supporting children's explorations of writing, both at home and in the classroom, and strive to find ways to do so that are both effective and manageable. As Doake (1988) points out,

> Teachers today have a second responsibility: they must also educate parents. In the past, they directed virtually all their attention to the children they were teaching, communicating only occasionally with parents in a newsletter or at a parent/teacher meeting. Now, they must give the parents their professional attention as well, to help them understand their role in the [academic] development of their children. (p. 76)

This book is our attempt to help teachers with this "second responsibility" to the parents of the children who share their classrooms.

When parents are effectively informed and actively involved they are in a position to work *with* you; when they're not, misunderstandings inevitably occur and opportunities for support and learning are sadly lost. We need to assist parents to understand what they can do at home to extend and enrich their child's learning experiences. Just as importantly, we need to learn from them what we can do to make the classroom offerings more closely match the needs and interests of their children. When allies work toward shared goals, the task is lightened and success is more likely.

The premise upon which this book is based is that teachers have as much to gain from open lines of communication as do parents. Fundamentally, we are looking for ways to initiate and maintain a positive two-way exchange. To this end, our book includes:

- Descriptions of a variety of ways of making information accessible and appealing to parents.
- Descriptions of the strategies, insights, and understandings revealed by young children as they interpret and come to terms with the complexities of our writing system.
- Writing samples and examples for teachers to use when explaining writing development to parents.
- Suggestions as to how parents can support their children's writing at home.
- Hints and guidelines for involving parents in the classroom.
- Handouts ready to be reproduced and shared with parents.
- A resource list of books we have found particularly helpful and informative about children's writing.

Although we've attempted to offer a rich selection of strategies and ideas, it's important to stress that they're meant only as suggestions and possibilities. It is essential that you tailor your *own* approach. We urge you to pick and choose and feel free to adapt and modify any and all of the ideas that follow to reflect your personal teaching style and the needs and interests of *your* parents and children. By the same token, teachers should not try to implement all of these techniques in any one year; to do so would be unnecessary and unsustainable. The key lies in a personal selection that achieves a manageable and workable balance that works for you and for the parents of the children you teach.

Writing is so much more than spelling, printing, and the mechanics of grammar. It involves expressing ideas and feelings, composing, organizing, problem solving, and reaching an audience. As used in this book, the term "writing" implies all of these dimensions.

Parents' Concerns About Children's Writing

All I know is his employers aren't going to put up with him *inventing* his spelling. He'll have to invent his own paycheck!

We are all aware that the inability of many students and adults to write and spell competently is a contentious issue in our society. Unfortunately, for too many people the word "spell" conjures up a great deal of anxiety. Gentry (1987) goes so far as to call "Spel" a four-letter word. In spite of their best intentions, many parents—and some teachers—manage to create this uneasiness and inadvertently inhibit children's writing by insisting too soon on the use of correct printing, spacing, punctuation, grammar, and conventional spelling. Because of widespread concern for spelling brought about by the back-to-basics movement and media reports of falling literacy standards, we need to assure parents that children *are* learning to spell through writing and that we're just as concerned as they are that children master the conventions.

Having been brought up with the weekly spelling test and regular drills on grammar, I am a good speller and grammar is important to me. It has helped me all my life and helped me get and hold jobs. I worry that my child isn't going to have that advantage.

Parents quite correctly value spelling ability and are understandably concerned that "new" approaches may be neglecting it:

I'm not really comfortable with this laid-back approach to spelling. I just can't see how kids can learn to spell if they don't memorize the correct spelling from the very beginning.

When writing is a major curriculum focus, teachers will find parents often ask questions of the following sort:

- Why don't you correct their spelling errors?
- If he can read these words, why can't he spell them?
- If you gave the class weekly spelling lists, wouldn't that help them spell the words correctly in their other writing?
- Do you still teach them how to correctly print the letters?
- Why don't you use workbooks? I bought him a phonics workbook and he does two pages every night. He loves it.
- Are the skills actually being taught?
- Is my child writing as well as she should be for her age?

- Do you encourage them to write on the computer?
- What can we do at home to help?

It's critical that these questions be aired, shared, and addressed. Because we know all too well how difficult it can be to come up with appropriate answers on the spur of the moment, we've included responses we've found helpful at relevant points throughout the book.

Figure 1-1 *Child's view of parent-teacher conference*

TWO

Teachers' Concerns About Involving Parents

*"Education is a very human partnership.
It depends for its strength, to a great degree, on how
teachers and parents feel about each other and
what they do to meet each others needs."* Rich, 1988

Although the benefits of parental participation have long been recognized, some teachers legitimately have a number of reservations and practical concerns about inviting parents into the classroom. Understandably, teachers can feel vulnerable and many hesitate to expose themselves to the scrutiny of adults who may not understand or be in sympathy with the teaching approach practised. Quite naturally, they shy away from situations that might leave them open to criticism, or at least having to explain and defend the way they do things. Awkward situations can arise if a parent works with a child (either at home or while assisting in the classroom) in a way that contradicts the teacher's approach. As James (1989) notes, "involvement of parents requires a high level of trust that parents will perform teaching activities skillfully and appropriately. Some teachers perceive that parents do not have such skills, and therefore there is a risk that parent involvement will counteract the teacher's work" (p. 33). For example, if the teacher encourages constructive spelling* but the parent corrects every error in a well-intentioned effort to help, the children will only be confused. Similarly, as the following incident illustrates, efforts by parents to teach

---

*The terms 'constructive,' 'functional,' and 'invented' spelling are used interchangeably. Please refer to the Glossary, p. 121 for a definition. The term 'invented' spelling is used in the handouts intended for the parents as it's likely to be the more familiar term.

don't always produce the desired or expected results. After a class trip to gather apples for an apple jelly cooking project, one of the children drew a picture of an apple tree.

Trying to capitalize on what appeared to be a "teachable moment," the child's mother, who was helping in the class at the time, decided to show her how to write "apple jelly." Slowly and carefully she named each letter in turn, directing her child to write the letters as she did so.

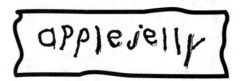

Pleased with the product, the parent then asked her daughter to write the phrase again and was mystified when the letters the child produced bore little relationship to the ones just dictated.

The teacher, who had observed the incident, made a mental note of the need, at a suitable time, to credit the parent's efforts but also to point out how important it is that instruction match the child's level of understanding. This parent had assumed that giving the child the correct spelling was all that was needed for the words to be learned; the child, however, still had many more discoveries to make about how writing works before such instruction would make sense. Although potentially problematic and often frustrating, such in-context, on-the-spot incidents provide invaluable opportunities for teachers and parents to become aware of topics that need clarification.

Confidentiality can be an issue as well. There is always the concern that children will be compared and their behavior judged and discussed in ways that can intrude on their privacy and that of their families. This issue must be dealt with diplomatically but directly. Ideally, expectations regarding confidentiality should be presented matter-of-factly and discussed openly before problems can occur.

Another inhibiting factor is fear of encroaching on the work of teaching assistants and clerical staff; teachers are wary of, and warned against, using parents to do jobs that otherwise would be given to paid employees. If restrictions are placed on the types of roles parents are permitted to assume in your school, it's still possible to invite parents in to observe and share their knowledge of their child with you.

Some teachers worry that parents might attempt to impose their ideas and tell them how to do their jobs. Others recognize that they will probably feel constrained and inhibited in the presence of an adult 'audience' and that these feelings could result in an uncharacteristic reluctance to "perform" as they usually do when, for example, dramatizing a story (e.g., "My what big TEETH you have, my Dear!!!!") or joining in during gym (What teacher wants to be seen doing a forward roll in front of parents?). Some teachers feel that children behave differently (either positively or negatively) when their parents are present and that this introduces an additional variable they'd rather not deal with.

> Sure, I want to involve the parents, but let's face it, there's only so many hours in a day . . . and my first responsibility is to the children, not the parents.

Teaching is an increasingly demanding and complex undertaking. Teachers often exhaust themselves trying to meet the needs of children who are grappling with the effects of poverty, divorce, transience, alcohol and drug abuse, and abusive or neglectful home situations. Sometimes the thought of trying also to meet the needs of parents who are themselves beleaguered by those same conditions utterly overwhelms. To complicate matters further, it's not uncommon for teachers to face classes composed of children from many different cultural backgrounds, some of whom have no proficiency at all in the language of instruction. As if that wasn't enough, many parents are functionally illiterate and teachers cannot be at all sure that the notes, pamphlets, and report cards sent home by the school are always understood. It's not difficult to understand why teachers who are faced with such an array of complicating factors might hesitate about embarking on a program to involve parents in the classroom. Ironically, it's precisely when teachers have to deal with such challenging situations that parent involvement is most needed, and the payoffs and benefits most likely to accrue. Research is reassuring on this point. After citing and reviewing numerous studies on the topic, Fullan (1991) forcefully states: "It is especially important to note that parent involvement practices succeed with less-educated parents and disadvantaged students, *where it is crucial that the school make a difference*" (p. 235, emphasis added). We are most in need of allies when things are difficult; parents are a source of support, assistance, and affirmation that we just can't afford not to tap.

If parents face overwhelming personal needs then they are not likely to become actively involved and, as teachers, we need to respect and understand this. Nevertheless, the invitation to participate in one way or another needs to be extended to all parents. A few extra minutes spent with the family of a new arrival to acquaint them with ways they can become involved can't help but make them feel welcome. Parents of your ESL children will particularly appreciate any extra care taken to provide additional explanations and clarifications if they are needed. They might not feel confident enough to participate, but they will know what is available and will have a greater understanding of their child's classroom situation. Our experience has shown us that many of these parents welcome the involvement and contacts outside the home that the school can provide. When reaching out to parents—all parents—the secret to successful communication is awareness of their situation and sensitivity to their needs.

The Tyranny of Time

In practical terms, including parents means an additional outlay of time and energy—neither of which teachers have to spare. We are the first to acknowledge this. It does take time, but this is time wisely invested. When parents are successfully involved, the rewards are many. Teaching can actually become easier. We've found that inviting parents on board almost always results in:

- a reduction of stress for all involved, because the openness generates feelings of cooperation and mutual respect.

- an exchange of information, some of which, although seemingly incidental at the time, may turn out to have significant implications for a teacher's response to particular children and the way things are done in the classroom.

- the evaluation process becoming more meaningful for parents because they have a frame of reference that enables them to better interpret the comments made during the parent-teacher conferences and written on report cards.

- the sharing and pooling of resources that might otherwise have gone unrecognized. (For example, one parent, a professional illustrator, demonstrated for the children how he created illustrations to accompany his published poems; a mother, recently arrived from China, scribed each child's name in Chinese characters on bookmarks while they watched; another came in faithfully week after week to listen to the children read.)

- children gaining in all sorts of ways from the consistency of a coordinated effort.

While it would be dishonest to deny that problems can arise, it is important to stress that most problems can be solved, and that the benefits of opening the classroom to parents far outweigh the negatives. Time invested in finding ways to involve and include parents can, in the long run, save time. Our experience has confirmed that parents quickly become allies and sources of support (and sometimes lasting friends) and that an open-door policy and invitations to participate pay unanticipated dividends. After a comprehensive review of the research on parent involvement, Fullan (1991) concludes: "the evidence shows, once teachers and parents interact on some regular basis around specific activities, mutual reservations and fear become transformed, with positive results for the personal and academic development of students and for parent and teacher attitudes" (p. 237). The strategies described in the following pages are intended to help teachers avoid the pitfalls and capitalize on the positives.

THREE

Visiting the Writing Classroom

*The classroom we envision
"resembles a wonderful busy
workshop rather than a theater full
of silent spectators."* MICKELSON, 1990

When parents visit the school, they find out firsthand that their child's classroom is probably quite different from the ones they themselves experienced as students. Classrooms are as individual as the teachers in them. The following description is a composite based on primary classrooms we know where teachers are attempting to bring writing to life for their children. A composite permits us to profile the ideal and highlight the best; as we all know, however, the day-to-day reality sometimes falls short. One of the most endearing qualities of human beings is that their reach frequently exceeds their grasp. Good teachers characteristically aim high and work hard to turn visions and goals into practice. We recognize, though, that no one has it all together all the time. Our description is therefore a pastiche of things we've seen in many different classrooms and a vision of what we'd like to see in more of them.

A child-written sign on the door similar to the one shown in Figure 3–1 not only says "Welcome," but signals to visitors that this is a classroom where children's early attempts at writing are respected. Writing is everywhere—child-authored stories, drafts, reports, messages, signs, labels, and books adorn the walls and are arrayed on shelves and stacked on tables throughout the room. Large tables provide work space; where tables aren't available, desks are pushed together to create work surfaces. Seating is strategically arranged so that the children are able to discuss

Figure 3-1 *This sign was written by a seven-year-old veteran of the class*

their thoughts, plan together, and be of assistance to each other. Consideration is given to comfort—cushions, an easy chair (a rocker is a popular choice, with adults and children alike), or a donated couch are tucked into a quiet corner. Carpets make it possible for children to work on the floor. The teacher's work area is no longer a desk but a large table where children can come for conferencing and parents can draw up a chair.

Storage is orderly, attractive, and accessible to both adults and students. Exercise books, writing folders, and portfolios are stacked together within easy reach. Portfolios are filed in alphabetical order by the child's name so that retrieval provides exposure and practical experience with alphabetization. Writing tools (sharpened pencils, felt pens, rulers, crayons, stic-kee notes, staplers, hole-punchers, date and draft stamps, file folders, word processors and printer, high-quality software, typewriter, etc.) are readily available. Individual pencil boxes (food storage containers made of heavy plastic without lids work admirably) are kept in the child's own storage cubby, table tray, or desk.

A special area is set aside as a writing center, but writing activity is certainly not limited to it. A variety of papers (in different shapes, sizes, colors, textures, and weights), blank booklets, and materials suitable for making book covers are offered. Resourcefulness and independence are encouraged from the beginning. Nearby, for easy reference, are a variety of charts: alphabet charts illustrating correct letter formation, word banks, song lyrics, poems, and monthly calendar pages filled in by the children. Some have been prepared or purchased by the teacher; others are clearly the work of the children; some are joint creations intermingling the writing of the teacher with that of the students. Copies of recently published

A relaxed, comfortable atmosphere facilitates genuine sharing.

student newspapers are hung by rings on the wall, and child-written booklets, birthday lists, and captioned photo albums recording field trips and special events are available for consulting and sharing. A message board (available to anyone who wishes to use it) and a mailbox are popular features. A sign stating *Somebody Would Like to Get a Note from You Today* hangs above a notepad, to which a pencil is attached with a cord. Parents are invited to write notes to their children, and the children are encouraged to write to anyone they wish in the school. (See the sample in Figure 3–2.) Notes can be delivered directly or "mailed" for weekly distribution. If need be, note distribution is unobtrusively monitored by the teacher to ensure that no child is consistently overlooked, or that hurtful messages are sent.

Instruction takes many forms, ranging from focused whole- or small-group activities (e.g., helping the class compose, record, and proofread the

Materials are more likely to be used if they are attractive and accessible.

"Daily News"), to needs-group problem-solving sessions (e.g., brainstorming with three children who are struggling to get their writing started), to on-the-fly individual conferences. The children are surrounded with models of good literature and shown how to look at books with a writer's eye. Demonstrations, in the context of meaningful writing activities, of the skills needed to accomplish those activities are routinely and systematically provided.

A feeling of warmth and acceptance characterizes the classroom. Children and adults work side by side at a relaxed pace. Informal and flexible groupings are the norm. During periods set aside for writing, some children will work with a partner, some will prefer to work alone, and others will be assisted by a visiting parent. Children are encouraged to see themselves as generators and creators of materials and each other as resources. On a good day, the room hums with purposeful activity; ideas

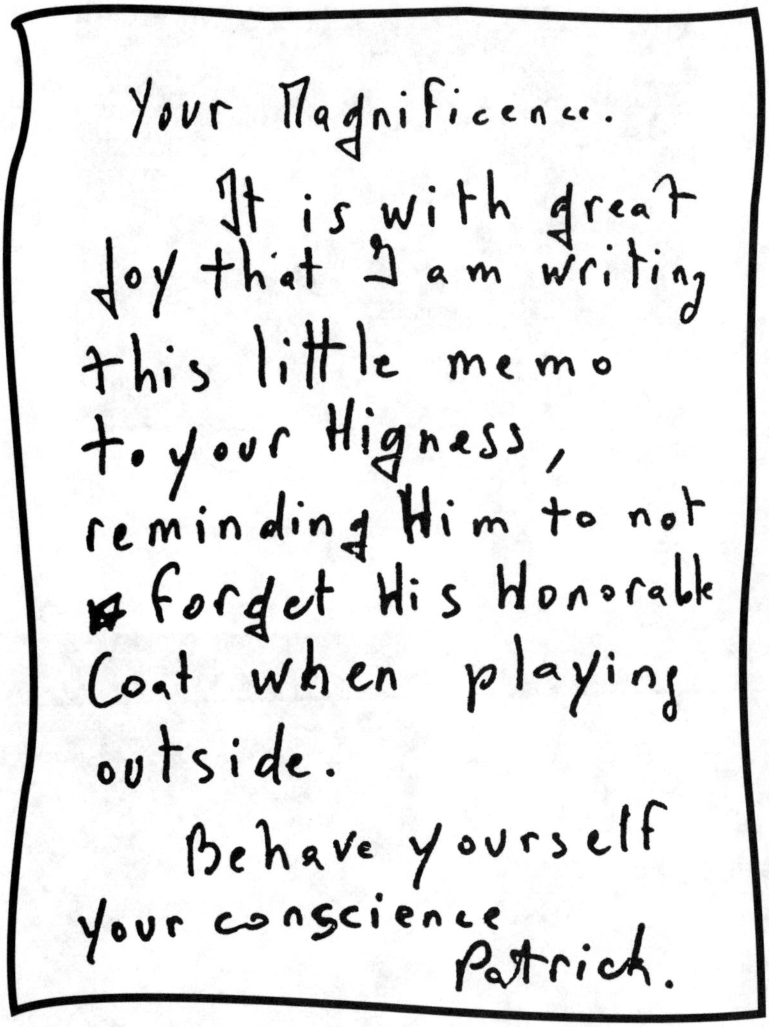

Your Magnificence.

It is with great Joy that I am writing this little memo to your Higness, reminding Him to not forget His Honorable Coat when playing outside.

Behave yourself Your conscience

Patrick.

Figure 3-2 *A playful note from a father to his son*

are freely discussed, questioned, and challenged, and everyone is a participant. Talk is valued and recognized as a tool for learning. Opportunities for talking, reading, and writing are front and center throughout the day and woven into every subject area. Quiet times are built into the daily schedule so that children have periods when they can read and think and write without distraction.

Individuality is respected and each child is provided with opportunities to write about things that personally interest and excite them. Because they're working on topics and projects they've had a say in

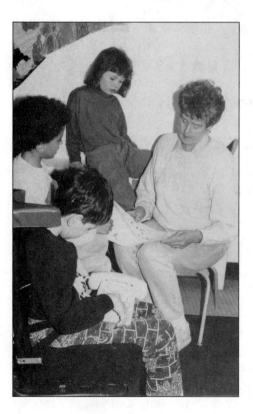

Groupings are flexible, fluid, and fit the task.

selecting, children take pride in their work, viewing it as *theirs*. All are invited to, and most are eager to, share their writings with their classmates. Sharings range from brief, informal consultations and requests for assistance, to small-group, peer editing/response sessions, to presentations for the whole class, and sometimes for others in the school. Affirmations are genuine and frequent, and the children are shown in numerous, concrete ways that their efforts are valued and respected. Their writings are not marked in the traditional red-pencil sense, but instead responded to and discussed. Feedback from the teacher is specific and personalized; children share the responsibility for deciding which aspects of their writing they need to focus on next and what needs to be worked on. Strengths are acknowledged and goals set. When work is displayed (only after permission to do so has been granted by the student), care is taken to mount and present it effectively. Students are involved in creating these displays, and the goal is to make their work accessible to others in the classroom and school. Personal journals are available to be read and reread, either privately or with a friend. Child-authored books constitute an important component of the classroom library, and they're shared and circulated in library-book fashion. Of course, a rich, varied, and regularly replenished supply of trade and reference books forms the foundation of the writing program.

Many schools have set up a publishing center; sometimes this is located in the library, but often it's squeezed into a corner of the room that houses the copy machine. All that's necessary are space, writing materials, simple bookbinding materials, and willing hands. If funding is available, a word processor and printer, a coil binder, and a laminator are excellent additions. Parent committees usually are open to supporting and raising funds for the creation of a publishing center.

Although a writing center is a feature of these classrooms, writing is not restricted to it. We've found that the math corner, the science center, the news table, the puppet theater, the felt-board, and the dramatic play center also inspire young children to write. Writing about their observations, experiments, and discoveries provide opportunities for children to gain valuable exposure to, and needed experience with, the nonfiction genres. As they record their findings, they learn the rudiments of concept mapping, list making, graphing, and report writing.

Writing is an integral part of each day's activities. Over the course of a single school day young children, either individually or in collaboration with others, may use writing:

- to sign the attendance sheet; to sign and date library cards
- to create a recipe, poem, riddle, song, or story
- to record significant events on a personal calendar
- to list questions to ask a guest speaker

Children write what is important to them:"Postponed Due to Accident."

- to write a thank-you letter to a parent who helped with a field trip or send get-well wishes to a sick classmate
- to advertise a lost item or favorite book
- to invite parents to a school event
- to add an entry to their journals or learning logs
- to label projects, caption artwork, or create props for a play
- to list needed items and record directions
- to record their opinions
- to report on research (e.g., "Facts About Whales")

The list could go on and on. The point is that children are exploring a wide range of genre and *using* writing for a variety of purposes *they* recognize as legitimate and meaningful, in the context of the on-going activities of the curriculum. When we think back on our own schooling and recall the penmanship exercises, assigned topics, and copying from the board that represented "writing" for us, we can easily appreciate just how much things have changed. If parents have not spent time in an elementary school since their own school days, it's hardly surprising if they react as if in unfamiliar territory.

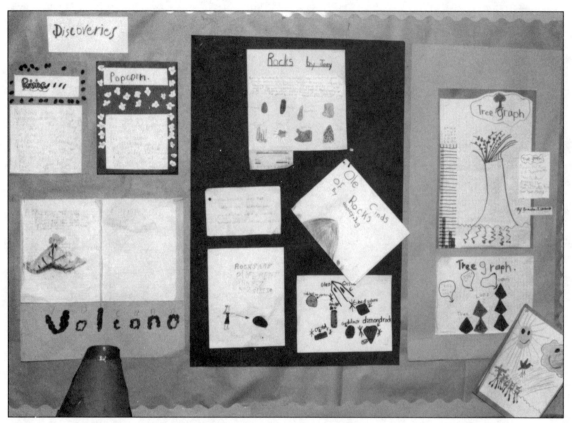

Lists, graphs, and fact sheets reflect the children's familiarity with expository forms.

Getting Off to a Good Start

"Children want to write. They want to write the first day they attend school. This is no accident. Before they went to school they marked up walls, pavement, newspapers with crayons, chalk, pens or pencils. . . anything that makes a mark. The child's marks say, 'I am.'" GRAVES, 1983

Before the First Day Starts

Welcome . . .
Come and Visit Your
Child's New Classroom

I'm going to be at school, getting the classroom (Room ___) ready for the new school year on

_____

(Specify day in week prior to school opening.)

Please feel free to bring your child and have a look around. Often an informal visit before school starts can ease anxieties and make the transition into a new classroom much happier and more comfortable. I am really looking forward to spending this time with you and to working with you in the year ahead. This invitation is extended to any other adults important to your child. Please don't hesitate to bring them along.

Sincerely,

Figure 4-1 *Visiting the classroom before school begins can allay anxieties*

Where it is possible to arrange it, invite parents and students to visit the school before the school year begins. Meeting their teacher and finding out about the classroom helps children ease into the new year. Invitations of this sort are common practice in Kindergarten; we feel they should be extended to children in all the primary grades.

Parents also welcome the opportunity to become familiar with the classroom environment, satisfy their curiosity, and even allay some anxieties they might have about the situation their child is moving into. Increasingly, early primary teachers are working in multiage or family-grouped classes in which at least some of their students spend more than a single year in their care. In order to make the new entrants welcome, it is particularly important that they be invited to meet the teacher and visit the school prior to opening day. This saves the children from having to simultaneously deal with a new teacher, new classroom, and the "resident population," an experience that can be initially intimidating. It also gives the teacher a chance to informally meet the child's family in a relaxed way. Invitations can be mailed (see Figure 4–1), or if it's easier, extended by phone. The time required is easily balanced by the goodwill and rapport that result and the insights gained about the children and their families.

Opening Day

Everything we do should signal to parents that they are welcome, and have a role, in our classrooms—on the first day as well as throughout the year.

On the first day of school, an open-door policy can be launched by inviting parents into the classroom to assist children in getting settled. It smooths the whole process if, as they enter the room, they're given a sheet suggesting ways they might help. A list of this kind helps overcome the awkwardness some parents feel about their natural desire to stay with their child for a little while and their fear of being perceived as an overanxious or hovering parent. It gives them something concrete and helpful to do and it provides sorely needed assistance during an inevitably hectic period. Just as important, having parents present creates yet another opportunity for the informal contacts and exchanges that often prove the most significant. An example of a list we've found useful can be seen in Figure 4–2.

Every available surface in the classroom and hallways should advertise the children's art, their writing, and the projects they've created. Attractively displayed stories and child-captioned paintings saved from previous years can make a powerful visual statement regarding the expectations for the writing program. Photographs of children engaged in ongoing activities provide illustrations of the learning context. Bulletin boards can be imaginatively exploited to communicate in a vivid and informative fashion the range and nature of the writing activities undertaken and encouraged in your classroom. Self-esteem is enhanced when students are invited to take responsibility for displaying their work. During the year, children can be allocated a generous section of wall space to use in displaying

YOU'RE WELCOME TO STAY

"The journey of a thousand miles begins with a single step."
Lao-Tse

The first day of school can be a very hectic time. If you're free to stay for a little while I would welcome your assistance and I'm quite sure your child would feel more comfortable having your help getting settled. The children may need your help:
• finding name tags from the pocket chart.
• locating places to sit.
• finding storage cubbies and coathooks (these are labelled with the children's names).
• making sure their supplies are complete (a supply list is posted on the board).
• putting names or initials on *everything*, including lunch boxes, sweaters, jackets, and shoes.
• locating the bathroom.

Don't hesitate to lend a hand to any other child who looks as if he or she could use one.

You're welcome to stay as long as you wish, but please be sure to say good-bye to your child before you leave. Feel free to drop in at anytime to observe or just to chat. Your assistance will always be welcomed, as it has been today.

Thank you!

Figure 4-2 *The first day goes smoothly if parents are invited to help*

their creations. When thoughtfully set up, the environment itself will proclaim the child-centered philosophy of the classroom. Although parents might not make a point of mentioning it, the impact of such displays is powerful and lasting. The children's work creates a mood and indirectly conveys a tremendous amount of information about what young children can do and will be producing.

One way to highlight the importance you place on writing is to make sure that the materials and resources you make available to the children to support their writing are clearly in evidence. Pithy statements

Parents are fascinated by examples and descriptions of the evolution of writing growth such as the one displayed above this birthday graph.

encapsulating the essence or focus of current views of the writing process can be posted at appropriate places. Comments such as the following have evoked positive responses from adults who have visited our schools:

> To watch children writing is to see focused energy and intelligence at work; anyone who has done so cannot dismiss the products of that work as insignificant, deficient, wrong. (Kress, 1982, p. ix)

> What is one of the most valuable gifts we can give language users? We can litter their environment with enticing opportunities and guarantee them the freedom to experiment with them. (Harste, Woodward, & Burke, 1984, p. 27)

> Means must be found to ensure that all children's first experiences of reading and writing are purposeful and enjoyable. Only in this way will they be drawn into applying their meaning-making strategies to the task of making sense of written language. (Wells, 1981)

When posted alongside current displays of the children's written work, these accompanying commentaries can serve both to reassure and enlighten. We've found a *time-sampling*, such as the one featured in the photograph and in Figure 4–3, to be an invaluable tool. Figure 4–3 portrays sequenced samples of writing produced by one child between the ages of three and eight years, offering parents an easily understood overview of how writing evolves and is refined over time.

For the young child first entering school, confidence is boosted when, on the very first day, they can take home a sample of their own writing which they can read to an appreciative audience. (We are acutely aware that some children do not return to supportive homes; this is one of the prime reasons we feel it is so important to communicate with parents about ways they can encourage their children's learning). A simple booklet, made from a single folded page (see Figure 4–4; a blank form is included in Appendix C), has proven to be a popular first day writing project. The format guarantees success. When folded, the back page contains a note for parents explaining the significance of learning to write one's name— a task not always fully recognized for the achievement it is. The inside pages contain simple open-ended activities the teacher and parent can carry out with the children. A note needs to accompany these booklets home to make parents aware they include a page for them to complete with their child.

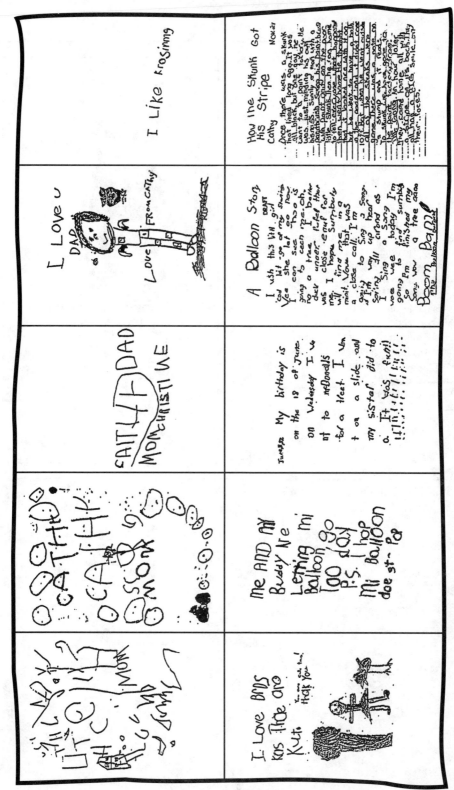

Figure 4-3 Progress over time is captured in a series of "freeze frames" (see Appendix B for enlarged version)

What's in a Name?

Learning one's own name, in written form, is a milestone event. The child's name is almost invariably the first written word learned. Usually, the initial letter is recognized and written first. Gradually, the other letters are learned, although sometimes their order is mixed and some are left out. By the time a child can write his name, he has already learned a lot about how written language works. He knows that particular letters in a particular order represent his name, and that the relationship between sound and symbol is not random. Being able to write his name and the names of family members, friends and classmates can be the entry point for learning how to write. It's an accomplishment that merits recognition.

This book was written by
chantelle

Age 5

September 27, 1992

Figure 4-4 *This simple booklet informs on several levels*

TOSE MI
FONSY

Jennifer
LauhEn

Teacher: The children can draw a picture and record their names and any other writing they wish to do. This becomes a record of the work done at the start of the year.

This is me and my teacher. We did math. We like to use the loft.

Parent: With your child you might like to record a highlight of his/her first day at school.

Formal and Informal Visits

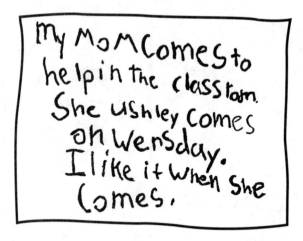

my MoM Comes to help in the class room. She ushley comes on Wensday. I like it when she Comes.

The initial weeks should be viewed as a period during which parents have the opportunity to become familiar with the classroom program and develop rapport with the teacher.

When you feel ready, invite parents to observe and assist in the classroom. A particularly effective way to introduce parents to your instructional program and approach is to schedule a personal observation for each parent early in the school year, but after the first general parent meeting (see Figure 4–5). These visits are offered to every parent on an individual basis and scheduled for anyone who requests one. This contrasts with extending a general invitation and then leaving it up to the parents to contact you with a request to come and observe; the advantage of the first approach is that more of the parents will actually elect to come. Visits to the classroom are particularly valuable for parents whose first language differs from the one spoken by the teacher, or for parents whose literacy skills may make it difficult for them to understand or interpret the newsletters and information pamphlets intended to explain the curriculum. For these parents, it makes a real difference if they can see for themselves how things are handled in the classroom.

Ideally, parents should be able to see you demonstrating writing with the children (e.g., scribing the morning news on the board while strategically calling on children for assistance with wording and spelling), and also observe the children independently engaged in writing. Observations become more meaningful if parents are provided with a handout suggesting areas they might want to focus on (See Figure 4–6).

Please Come and Observe

I would like to invite you to spend some time in our classroom (preferably a morning) so you can see what school is like for your child.

It would help me to know which day and date is most convenient for you. Please complete the form below and return it by _____ so I can schedule visits and confirm your request. If arranging this time is difficult, please let me know so we can work something out.

I am looking forward to spending this time with you, answering any questions you might have about our classroom, and discussing the goals you would like your child to work toward in the coming months.

_____
(Teacher's Signature)

------------------------------------ (Tear Here) ------------------------------------

The most convenient morning for me to visit the classroom is:
Monday ☐; Tuesday ☐; Wednesday ☐; Thursday ☐; Friday ☐

Comment: _____
_____
_____
_____
_____

_____   _____   _____
(Child's Name)   (Parent's Signature)   (Phone)

Figure 4-5 A *formal invitation says you're serious*

When the opportunity presents itself, parents can be invited to share any relevant information about their child (e.g., attitudes, learning style, physical coordination, concerns). Try to arrange to do this during center or choosing time when children are independently engaged; but we feel it only fair to warn you that sometimes the only free time available is recess.

A FOCUS FOR YOUR OBSERVATION

My child's name _____   Date_____
Visiting Parent(s) name(s)_____

Welcome to our class!
You might like to observe and comment on the following:

Your child's interactions with other children:

Your child's particular interests in the classroom and on the playground:

Your child's attitude toward learning:

How your child participates during whole-class group times:

Your child's attitude toward and involvement with writing:

Your child's response to books:

Something that surprised you about learning in this classroom:

Something special about your child's progress:

Please share your observations with your child.
                              We are looking forward to your next visit.

Figure 4-6 *Providing a focus can enrich a parent's observation*

This is an excellent opportunity to elicit and record a *few* major goals the parents have for their child and to inform them of your own aspirations for their child in the coming months. Figure 4–7 is a form that can be used to record the goals discussed. Later, when you come to write report cards, these forms prove invaluable as a reference and a reminder of what is important to the parents.

Each teacher is different and each will want to involve parents in different ways and to differing degrees. A great deal is gained when parents have the opportunity, if they feel comfortable doing so, to participate in ongoing activities. Many parents (but not all) want to become more actively involved in their child's schooling. It's important to recognize that, just as some teachers are apprehensive about involving parents, many parents are uneasy about assisting in the classroom. Some question whether they have anything to offer and worry that they will not know what to do. Others hesitate to help with children's writing when they don't feel

Focused observation helps parents appreciate accomplishments they might otherwise miss.

SETTING OUR SIGHTS ON SUCCESS

Name **Desmond**   Date **Sept 29**

Parent	Teacher
Plans and goals for my child:	Plans and goals for student:
− Write more extensively − Initiate writing activities on his own, − Continue to read with a positive attitude.	− To feel confident as a writer. − Become more of a risk taker − Maintain his excellent social skills.

Student's plans and goals:
− To read chapter books by himself
− To have "_lots_" of friends.

Figure 4-7 *Shared goal setting opens the lines of communication*
(*Completed form, see Appendix D for blank form*)

confident about their own writing skills—especially their spelling. Some are concerned about time commitments; for others, arranging or affording babysitting so as to free time to visit the classroom is an issue. Sometimes fathers, step-parents, and foster parents need to be assured that the invitation includes them. Efforts to involve parents will work only if these concerns are recognized and treated with empathy and consideration. Invitations to participate are more likely to be accepted if teachers are open and the welcome is genuine. Parents need to feel comfortable, welcomed, and needed if they are to play an active role in their child's school. We cannot expect them to be receptive to our suggestions if they do not feel at ease and appreciated.

Notes and newsletters, phone calls, orientation meetings, meet-the-teacher nights, open houses, curriculum fairs, and classroom visits to observe or assist, all have a role in familiarizing parents with the classroom organization, philosophy, and plans for the year.

Although informing parents is a crucial first step, our ultimate goal is to include and involve them. Invitations to participate should be offered and guidelines and expectations openly communicated. This is especially necessary for any parents who are assisting in the classroom. It is unfair to assume that parents will intuitively understand how we would like them to interact with the children. We should be prepared to model for them how to act as scribes for children; how to respond to content before focusing on mechanics; how to handle requests for spellings or react to "errors"; how to serve as editors and assist with publishing. These guidelines can be conveyed informally, but it is essential that they be conveyed clearly and concretely in a nonthreatening manner. Yates and Ryan's (1987) advice may prove helpful for parents:

> Talk about what has been said, how it is said and how it is organized. Try not to "jump in" too quickly when your child is writing. Encourage them to work on their own writing—don't do it for them. (p. xii)

There are many options for scheduling visits for parents to assist in the classroom. These can range from invitations to come in and help on a particular day at a specific time to an open invitation to drop in at any time convenient to the parent. Some teachers like to have different parents in the classroom every day; others limit parent participation to one or two days each week. It's up to you to decide what will be most productive in your particular situation. Many teachers reserve one day a week when there are no visitors. This is often treasured time and no teacher should ever feel guilty for savoring it.

However you choose to schedule visits and organize for participation, the important thing is to consistently do so and not to leave it to chance or serendipitous opportunity. Once parents have responded to requests for involvement it is vital that these be followed up—parents will tell you there is nothing so frustrating as responding to a request for participation only to have it unacknowledged. Figure 4–8 invites parents to participate and help in the classroom on an ongoing basis; Figure 4–9 suggests specific ways they can become involved. It works best if both forms are sent home at the same time.

Would You Like To Lend A Hand?

You are welcome to drop into the classroom anytime you wish to observe and participate in our ongoing activities. You can look forward to an interesting and rewarding experience, while at the same time learning firsthand about your child's schooling. The children's learning can be richly enhanced by the regular and ongoing involvement and contributions of parents such as yourselves.

I have attached a copy of our daily timetable with an indication of when your assistance would be especially appreciated.

I prefer to come on _____ at _____
                    (day of the week)   (time)

I am prepared to come:

once a week ☐;   once every two weeks ☐;   once a month ☐.

Comments:

_____

_____

_____

_____

------------   _____   _____
(Child's Name)   (Parent's Signature)   (Phone)

Figure 4-8 *Everyone gains when parents participate, especially the children*

There Are So Many Ways You Can Help!

Volunteers (Mothers, Fathers, Grandparents . . .) can add *so* much to the writing experiences of children in the classroom. There are *many* ways you can help. The following are simply some suggestions. Please indicate if any of these appeal to you and if and when you would be willing to join us to work on these activities. If your work schedule makes coming to the classroom difficult and you'd like to lend a hand anyway, please feel free to suggest how in the space below.

- Sharing with the children special skills, talents, hobbies, or job information to provide background knowledge for their writing.
- Reading to and with individual children, small groups, and/or the class. Reading supports writing in countless ways.
- Being an appreciative audience for students while they share and discuss their writing.
- Assisting the children with revising and proofreading.
- Helping children type and edit their stories onto the word processor.
- Publishing books (helping with layout, bookbinding).
- Helping children to design and create big books.
- Helping with our parent library.
- Selecting, circulating, and promoting the classroom library collection.
- Assisting in the computer lab.
- Sewing costumes, puppets, and feltboard figures for dramas and stories written by the children.
- Babysitting for other parents who are visiting the classroom.
- Helping stock and maintain the school's Parent Corner.
- Any other suggestions? _____

We all gain when we work together. Thank you for your willingness to share your time and talents.

_____   _____   _____
(Child's Name)   (Parent's Signature)   (Phone).

Figure 4-9 *Parental participation requires planning and preparation*

Parent Corner: A Place to Call Their Own

A trend we applaud in the design of new schools, and in the remodeling of existing ones, is the increasing consideration being given to providing a special space for parents. In some schools a separate room is set aside; in others, a small section in the library or an alcove off the main hallway is all that can be spared. Usually, a few comfortable chairs and a table are made available, along with a bulletin board, bookcase, and the fixings for coffee. Such an area can have multiple uses: it can house a parent lending library, provide a quiet corner for the reading of journal and magazine articles, and offer opportunities to view educational videos (some professionally produced, others created at the school). Busy parents especially appreciate having ready access to materials that inform them about their children's learning. As one working parent commented, "I have only used the library a few times, but knowing that it's available is a great comfort." (An annotated list of books about writing that parents have reported finding useful, which you may wish to refer to when developing a library for parents, is included in Appendix A.)

A parent corner is an ideal location for an information-exchange bulletin board to display items such as notices about upcoming children's events, visiting speakers, preschool programs, and baby-sitting requests. Teachers are not always comfortable having parents in the staff room during recess and lunch, and some parents are not at ease in what they perceive to be the teacher's territory. A parent corner concretely signals that parents are genuinely welcome in the school by providing a place they can call their own.

If the creation of a parent corner strikes you as an unrealistic demand to add to your already jam-packed schedule, may we stress that these areas are most successful when organized, stocked, and managed by the parents themselves. If your school has a Parents' Committee, this is one responsibility they are often more than willing to assume. When parents have a role in establishing a parent corner, they are more likely to feel a sense of ownership. If no such committee exists, a request sent to the parents of the children in your class will usually result in offers of help. Although it is important that you support a parent corner, and encourage parents to make use of it, you should not feel obligated to provide it all by yourself. No matter who sets it up, the key is that parents feel welcome, needed, appreciated, and part of the school.

An open-door policy reassures. It minimizes parents' concerns about not being included in their child's education beyond parent interviews, and lets them see the learning environment for themselves. A major benefit

Location counts. Items will be noticed and read if the board is placed where parents pick up their children.

of classroom visits is that they provide parents with a frame of reference; they are able to observe their child in the context of the other children. In the words of one parent, "I feel quite free to come by and ask questions about my child's progress and take part in the classroom program. It keeps things in perspective."

Juggling the demands of home and work makes it difficult for everyone to become involved. We need to guard against judging parents who do not, or cannot, participate; whatever their reasons are, we must accept and respect them as valid. It's important, though, that the opportunity to participate be extended to all parents, whether they choose to accept it or not. The particular needs of, and pressures on, working parents must be recognized. One way to accommodate them is by offering projects that can be undertaken whenever their schedules permit. Some are happy to volunteer for projects that can be worked on at home, such as making cushions for the reading corner or creating felt figure characters and puppets

Guidelines for Parent Participation

- *The aim is to involve and include, not to exploit.* Parents should be working with and for the children, not just washing the paint pots and holding hot dog sales. Remember the teacher's needs, although important, are not the prime reason for involving parents.

- *Involve as many parents as possible.* Try not to create an inner circle of parents who are called on repeatedly while others are rarely asked. Remember to include fathers, too.

- *Outline your expectations, giving clear guidelines.* Openly discuss and negotiate with parents their role and responsibilities.

- *Respect parents' competence and creativity.* Although guidelines are essential, leave tasks open enough so that parents can bring into play their own talents and abilities. Just as you would with children, involve parents in tasks worth doing, from which they can derive a sense of accomplishment.

- *Give credit where credit is due.* A word of thanks, a note of acknowledgement in the school newspaper, thank-you cards from the children, captions or labels thanking parent contributors under displays of special projects are always appropriate and always appreciated.

- *Don't talk down to parents.* Sometimes our efforts to be clear and understandable can inadvertently patronize .

- *Provide for physical comfort.* Little things mean a lot: show parents where they can hang their coats and leave personal belongings; point out the location of the staff bathroom; offer coffee.

- *Let the children know how much their parents' visits and contributions are valued.*

Figure 4-10 *Pragmatic points for successful participation*

to accompany the stories the children have written. One working mother commented, "It is a relief to be included even though my job makes it impossible for me to help in the classroom. I really got a kick out of the letter from the kids thanking me for the finger puppets I cut out for them."

The growing number of single-parent families calls for particular sensitivity on the part of the school. Parents who are separated or sharing custody really appreciate duplicate copies of children's newsletters, report cards, and other pertinent information, so both parents can be kept informed.

Parents who have had a positive experience with the classroom situation tend to act as goodwill ambassadors. They are more likely to endorse the philosophy of the teacher and thereby help alleviate any concerns that might be circulating. The key to successful participation is to avoid having the parents feel they are being used. (See the guidelines in Figure 4–10.) It is worth reminding ourselves that they are there to enrich the classroom experiences *of the children* and to gain insight into their own child's learning, not to subsidize the work of the classroom teacher.

FIVE

Meetings with Parents

◆

"The perception that when one writes one must spell correctly appears to be the single biggest constraint which 5- and 6-year-old children see as the reason why they can't engage in the process. Given the attention spelling is given by teachers and parents, this perception is understandable, but nonetheless dysfunctional to growth in literacy." HARSTE, WOODWARD, & BURKE, 1984

The acceptance of an integrated literacy-based curriculum, rather than a skills-oriented approach, requires a fundamental change in attitude for many parents. If parents are to be asked to alter what are often firmly entrenched views about how children learn, if changes in attitude as well as knowledge are to occur, then information needs to be presented *gradually* in a way that nurtures such changes and builds support for them. One means of accomplishing this is through informational meetings. We have found two to three meetings a year manageable (for both teachers and parents) and suggest holding the first early in September, the second close to the first reporting conferences, and, should you choose, to host a third one in January or February. Parents' meetings work best if:

- they focus directly on topics and issues of concern to the parents;
- parents have input into, and are consulted about, the agenda prior to the meetings;
- they are informal, but informative; and
- no one is patronized.

The specific focus of these meetings will depend on the concerns of your parent group, ages of your students, and the nature of your program. If you are working with early primary students, we strongly recommend that the first of these meetings specifically address writing and reading as parents have so many questions about these topics. The advantage of holding the meetings early in the term is that myths and misconceptions can be dispelled and concerns openly discussed. The advantage of spacing the meetings is that it gives parents time to reflect and to formulate and articulate their questions, knowing they have a forum where their questions will be addressed. The advantage of holding more than one meeting is that it makes it possible to deal with a range of curriculum areas and develop the topic of literacy acquisition in greater depth.

When addressing writing and spelling with a parent group, it is important that parents:

- are helped to recognize and appreciate the significance of children's early attempts at writing.
- be made aware of the successive discoveries about written language children make as they become increasingly competent and adept as writers.
- gain insights into the parallels between oral and written language and how both are acquired.
- understand the contribution reading and writing make to spelling.
- understand the value and role of functional spelling.
- view "errors" as informative indicators of the child's level of understanding.
- are made aware of how important it is that they be accepting rather than critical of their child's attempts to write.
- realize the importance of making time and opportunity for writing.
- be aware of the model they provide when they are spelling and writing with and for children.
- understand what they can do to support and enrich their child's explorations of writing within and beyond the classroom.

A comment needs to be made about the level of information presented. It is important that information shared with parents be accessible and easily understood. In seeking to achieve this, however, it is easy to make the mistake of overly simplifying or of offering explanations that are little more than superficial summaries or bland generalizations. The key is to find a way to be accessible, interesting, and yet genuinely informative. It is our obligation to make sure our meetings are worth coming to and that parents feel they've gained from being there. Let's not forget that, just as we do, parents also have to juggle tight schedules to free the time to attend.

Initial Informational Meeting with Parents

In our experience the most effective time for the first evening meeting with parents is as early in the school year as you can manage. If at all possible, this meeting should be in addition to Meet the Teacher Night, if your school hosts one, so that parents are not put in the position of having to juggle a number of agendas at once, which is almost inevitable if they have more than one child in the school. A program an hour or so in length seems to work best. The classroom is the first choice as a setting because it places the parents in the learning environment their children experience. This setting seems to relax parents and trigger questions and observations that are rooted in the specifics of what the children are doing. And children's books and writings are available to the teacher as concrete examples to illustrate any points being made. The library also can offer a congenial meeting place, but the echoing, cavernous gymnasium should be avoided.

Invitations need to be circulated at least a week ahead with a reminder sent home a day or two before (See Figure 5–1). If the children can handle it, they can write the invitations; if the writing is still beyond them, the children can personalize the invitations by illustrating them. We've found that parents are much more likely to attend these meetings if they are informed of the topics to be addressed and if their questions and concerns are elicited in advance and made part of the agenda. (Parents seem more willing to contribute suggestions if they can do so anonymously.)

The points made during the presentation can be effectively reinforced by conspicuous and attractive displays of children's writing. A time sampling—presenting selected samples of one child's writing from the first scribbles through the exploration and mapping of sound-symbol relationships to the skilled production and manipulation of conventional forms—makes a powerful and informative display. (One we've used successfully begins on page 101.) Hanging it in the hallway gives parents access to it and the opportunity to study it as long as they wish. When made into transparencies, these sequenced samples work admirably during parent meetings to focus and spark discussion and give parents insight into the hypotheses and strategies children work with as they try to make sense of our writing system. Should you wish to use it this way, a full-size version is included in Appendix B, along with suggestions for guiding the discussion.

Supporting Young Writers

Date : _____

Time: _____

Place : _____

Are you amused, bemused, confused by your child's writing? Then you won't want to miss our first class meeting, which will focus on:

The writing of young children

Invented or constructive spelling

How reading supports and enriches writing

Ways you can help your young writer

If you have any concerns or queries please jot them down on the tear off sheet below. Although this meeting will offer insights into your child's development, the progress of individual children will not be discussed at this time. I would appreciate it if this form could be returned in the next few days.

I am looking forward to spending this evening with you.

_____

(Teacher's Signature)

-------------------------------- (tear here) --------------------------------

Your Concerns and Queries?

Figure 5-1 *Soliciting parents' suggestions increases participation*

Of course, you may prefer to use example[s]
we encourage you to do so. This type of pr[e]
when a span of three or more years is repr[
Parents find it reassuring to see for then[
and standard forms evolve from early ex[
tions, and the intention to communicate.

Selections of written work done by t[he]
few weeks should be available to the parent[
own child's writing in terms of the informa[
meeting. It's been our experience that many [
ing in a totally new light after the presentatio[n
the first time the competence and percepti[
their own child's efforts to write. They begin to u[
formal instruction the young child is actively n[
including the world of print" (Harste, Woodwar[d
having captions on the art work and signs aroun[
children (see Figure 5–2), parents not only see t[

are p[
writin[
activ[

of th[
tune[
film[
info[
We'[
vari[
tive[
in t[
rea[
sh[

te[
sa[
o[
w[

Figure 5-2 *Children need to write for many different purposes*

TRANSLATION: My mom's doctor said that we were [are] having a m[
baby's heart beat.

oducing but also are provided with concrete examples of children
g for real-life reasons. Photographs showing the class involved in school
ties also can be displayed with child-written captions.

The presence of the school principal at this first meeting (and at all
em if it can be arranged) sends a powerful signal that he or she is in
with the approach practiced in the classroom. Professionally produced
or videos on the topic are an excellent means of providing background
rmation (these are often available from the district resource center).
e found a video or slide presentation of the present class involved in
ous reading and writing activities to be a particularly popular and effec-
way to communicate how the approach and philosophy are implemented
he classroom. Parents, especially those unable to attend the meetings,
lly appreciate being able to borrow these videos to view at home and
re with other family members.

Parents gain confidence when it's pointed out they have been mas-
teachers in their child's acquisition of speech and that by following the
me model, and creating similar conditions, they can guide their child
er the threshold to literacy. A comparison drawn between how oral and
itten language are learned portrays to parents the importance of:

- parental modeling,
- encouraging their child to freely explore the many uses of writing,
- appropriate responses to the child's attempts to communicate through writing, and
- the rationale behind an integrated approach to language and literacy that reflects a focus on meaning before form.

The parallel between the acquisition of competence in oral and written language are outlined in Figure 5–3. The table was created by Fields (1989), who stated: "Similar stages of talking and writing do not occur at the same ages, but they do occur in the same sequence" (p. 33). We've found that the table makes an informative transparency to share and discuss with parents. Parents react with recognition and a certain measure of relief when it becomes evident to them that their child's investigation and acquisition of writing in some ways parallels the acquisition of speech. It is well worth pointing out that just as babbling evolves into the expressive and fluent oral competence most children possess on entering school, squiggles and scribbles gradually lead to the confident handling of standard forms if appropriate support and experience are provided.

Comparable oral and written stages in language development		
Oral language	*Written language*	*Understanding level*
Babbling and cooing	Scribbling stage	Exploration of medium
Language intonation	Linear/repetitive stage	Refining the form
Native language sounds	Letter-like forms	Cultural relevance
Words	Letters and early word-symbol relationships	Conventions of language
Creative grammar	Invented spelling	Overgeneralization of "rule" hypotheses
"Adult speech"	Standard spelling	Formal structure

Figure 5-3 *Comparison of oral and written language development*

If parents return the Concerns and Queries portion of the meeting announcement form (See Figure 5–4), it's important that these questions be addressed or acknowledged. Parents should feel free to raise questions at any point in the presentation, and time should be left at the end of the evening for other questions that might come up. Many of the questions noted in the section "Parents' Concerns About Children's Writing" in Chapter 1 will be asked at this time. What follows is a sampling of common questions, along with some comments you might find helpful in responding to them.

(tear here)
Your Concerns and Queries?

I would like more information on the multi-age class way of teaching & on how children are taught to write.
Will French be taught in Gr. 1?

Pat Bell

Figure 5-4 *Inviting input communicates respect*

Are the skills actually being taught?

Yes, yes, and yes again . . . and better than ever! Although educational philosophy and practice reflects some dramatic shifts, the goal that schools produce students who are confident and skilled readers and writers has not changed. A fear that teachers are implementing a laissez-faire approach, where students are allowed to do, or not do, whatever they choose, frequently underpins this question. Thus, it's very important to spend a little time explaining that, while the teacher's role has changed, students are most certainly provided with instruction, models, demonstrations, specific and systematic guidance, and many opportunities to practice, develop, and refine their communication and literacy skills.

The key point is that teachers are now attempting to teach skills in the context of relevant, real-life experiences. For example, rather than having young children complete a fill-in-the-blank worksheet to identify the beginning sounds of a series of unrelated objects (an activity with no real-life counterpart), teachers will instead draw children's attention to the sounds used to represent words by engaging them in writing a letter or recording the daily news. The advantage is that children learn the utility and relevance of the skill, as well as where and how to apply it. Skills learned in context are more easily learned and retained, even though the activities the children undertake are far more challenging and engaging than the skills exercises and drills that used to dominate the curriculum. So, yes, the skills certainly are being taught, but they're approached differently, for the reason so eloquently conveyed by Katz's (1991) warning: "When we teach skills to children too early, too formally, and out of context, they will learn them without the desire to ever use them again" (p. 17).

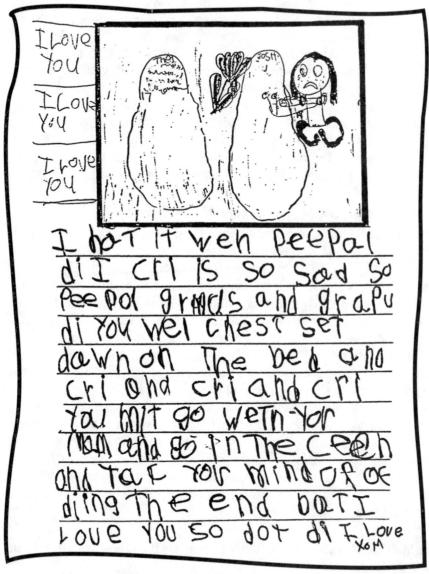

TRANSLATION: I hate it when people die. I cry. It's so sad. Some people's grandmas and grampas die. You will just sit down on the bed and cry and cry and cry. You might go with your mom and go in the cemetery and take your mind off of dying. The end. But I love you so don't die I love you. [Mom? or XOX?]

Why don't you correct their spelling mistakes?

The "errors" in young children's writing are regarded not as mistakes but rather as intelligent attempts, or approximations. It's assumed that the child has represented the word as best he or she is able to at that time. There is little to be gained, and a great deal to be jeopardized, if these efforts are met with criticism and constant correction. When children are overly concerned about errors, they tend to play it safe and use only the words they're sure of getting correct, or they avoid writing altogether. Sadly, they thus cut themselves off from the very experiences that would help them become better spellers and writers. Recent "insights into risk-taking and its relationship to literacy and literacy learning suggest that literacy programs which emphasize correct responses and attempt to eliminate error fail to best serve literacy learning" (Harste, Woodward, & Burke, 1984, p. 136). As Graves and Stuart (1985) point out, it's worth reminding ourselves "of the reason why spelling exists: so that people may write" (p. 168).

Does this mean teachers don't care about correctness?

Certainly not . . . but it's a matter of timing and ownership. We want all children to first direct their attention to content and ideas—to the meaning of what they're trying to say—without feeling constrained by their ability to spell conventionally. Standard spelling is important, however, if meaning is to be effectively communicated. To this end, children are surrounded by models of convention and correctness (reading is a powerful resource for information about spelling) and encouraged to be analytical and attentive to the way words are constructed, but in the context of "real" reading and writing. If we do all the "correcting" of children's work, we take the proofreading responsibility out of their hands and deprive them of "the essential problem-solving and confidence-building experiences that come from inventing their own spellings and working through the writing process themselves" (Villiers, 1989, p. 2). Emphasis on proofreading increases as children gain experience and confidence with writing. As soon as they can handle it, they are encouraged to draft and revise certain selected pieces, first creating a working copy, which they then edit for content and proofread for spelling and mechanics.

Wouldn't weekly spelling lists help them spell the words correctly in their writing?

Not necessarily. There's a great deal of evidence that children will correctly spell the words on weekly spelling quizzes, yet use functional spellings for those same words in their writing—sometimes on the same page. Transfer

TRANSLATION: I am going to the police station and I am going fast.

appears to be made difficult because the list words are often an arbitrary assortment, presented out of context and learned by rote. Despite widely held beliefs to the contrary, this is neither an efficient nor an effective way to learn to spell. Happily, many teachers are finding more productive ways of drawing children's attention to the intricacies of spelling.

You might like to direct parents to *Spel . . . Is a Four-Letter Word*, by J.R. Gentry; in succinct, compelling prose he addresses many of the questions parents raise about spelling.

If she can read these words, why can't she spell them?

There's a difference between production and recognition. Most adults can read *many* words they may not be able to spell correctly. This is partly because, in English, it's possible to represent the same sounds in many different ways. Consequently, although your child may certainly be able to read a word, either by working out the sounds or inferring it from the context, that does not mean she will be able to generate its standard spelling. Her version may reflect the sounds heard, but because there are a variety of ways to represent those sounds, it might not match the conventional or correct option.

Why don't you use worksheets?

Worksheets tend to isolate skills and offer decontextualized drills and exercises; they are rarely engaging, enriching, or genuinely instructive. In a scathing analysis, Frank Smith (1986) dismisses the activities typically offered by worksheets and workbooks as "decontextualized, fragmented, and trivial . . . .The activities have no immediate utility, relevance, or sense, and they do not create the kind of situation in which children normally and sensibly learn" (p. 98). Children learn far more when given opportunities to explore written language by writing stories, reports, poems, songs, opinion polls, letters, announcements, etc. While there's no argument that a judiciously selected worksheet can occasionally provide useful practice, a steady diet of them serves as a poor model of what writing involves. Worksheets place children into passive roles as responders and repliers; genuine writing opportunities, in contrast, help them become initiators, producers, problem solvers, and creators. Worksheets are rarely worthy of the children who are asked to complete them.

Do teachers still teach children how to correctly print the letters?

Yes. The teacher models and demonstrates letter formation every time she or he writes in front of the children, sometimes commenting specifically on letter formation, sometimes not. Wall charts illustrating the letters are hung where they can be easily referred to. Although teachers nowadays rarely insist that all children make their letters in precisely the same fashion, they are certainly alert to noticing and then intervening to assist children who are producing inefficient, ineffective, or awkward hand movements.

If my child is uninterested in writing, should I be worried?

Children are individuals; some will be intrigued by writing from their first encounter with a crayon, while others will seem indifferent or oblivious. One way to heighten a young child's interest in writing is to make it a vital component of play. For example, if trucks and cars are an attraction, set up a pretend garage with props that invite writing. These might include booklets of gasoline coupons; work-order books, complete with carbons; signs announcing giveaways with a fill-up; bills; receipts; and money. Similarly, make-believe hardware or sports equipment stores, fix-it shops, banks, optometrists' and doctors' offices can easily be created by means of a few signs and creative scrounging. If stocked with the sorts of "literacy props" actually used in those settings (prescription pads, deposit slips, bank books, price tags, labels, sale signs, eye charts, typewriters, order forms, etc.), children will incorporate writing into their play—and learn a great deal about writing in the process. Elaborate props are not needed; children often prefer blank forms and booklets that they can transform themselves. It's important to find ways to entice and invite children to engage in writing that they perceive to be pleasurable and low risk. Play can accomplish this masterfully. It would be a mistake to communicate your concern to your child, or to start putting pressure on him to write.

How do you teach writing to children who are just learning English?

The first thing is to ensure that ESL children are helped to feel comfortable and accepted in our classrooms. Proficiency in their own language should be acknowledged and supported. All children need a rich exposure to oral language before they can be expected to explore and experiment with writing; for children faced with acquiring a second language, oral exposure is critical. "Children cannot be expected to spell words correctly, if they have not heard them, cannot pronounce them and cannot read them" (Tarasoff, 1992). Time to listen, speak, and be read to are vital prerequisites, and time spent this way will ultimately support writing development.

Play props invite and support the creating and telling of stories; they are also great fun!

Collaborative composing on the computer enriches the writing experience.

Do you encourage them to write on the computer?

Yes. The word processor is a marvellous tool, and it's the writing implement of today and of the future. There are some excellent word processing programs specifically designed for young children that make it easy for them to gain productive access to the computer. For some children, transcribing their letters is a laborious and frustrating exercise; keyboarding can free them from that so that they are able to direct their attention to composition. Editing and proofreading are made far easier for older children by the cut-and-paste capacity of the computer and by the avail-ability of spell-checkers and the thesaurus. Similarly, access to spell-checkers appears to heighten awareness of, and encourage, correct spelling. There's no question that access to computers can enrich and extend children's experience of writing.

SUPPORTING YOUNG WRITERS

A Parent's Guide

© A. Preece and D. Cowden, 1992

" Writing is learned by writing, by reading, and by perceiving oneself as a writer. . . . Writing is fostered rather than taught. . . . What is required is an understanding is of what a child faces in learning to write."   Frank Smith, 1982

Parents who want their children to read and write must read and write themselves -- and talk about the experience."
Graves and Stuart, 1985, p.198 .

Figure 5-5 *An informative handout will become a reference that's relied on* (See Appendix E *for duplicating and folding instructions*)

QUESTIONS YOU MIGHT   BE ASKING YOURSELF

So, what's different?

Children used to be taught to write by copying letters, words and sentences from the board, and by tracing-over and writing under a teacher-prepared model:

My name is Jane

My name is Jane

We now realize these methods actually interfered with the free exploration essential for real understanding. Children learn best if they are permitted to set their own pace and pursue their own interests while being gently guided and challenged. As young children begin to explore and understand how writing 'works' they typically produce, in rough succession:

• free scribbling

• scribbling that resembles lines of writing

• letter-like forms

• letters mixed with memorized or copied words

• 'invented' or 'functional' spellings

-- all the while more closely approximating
   standard spelling and form.

Children must first discover writing as a tool for communicating meaning; concern with correctness should come later. Consequently in today's classroom, instead of dutiful copying you will find children productively engaged in writing:

• comic strips, captions on their art work
• notes, notices, signs, and posters
• letters and announcements
• journals, stories and reports
• charts, maps, and directions
• rules for games, slogans
• newspapers, riddle and joke books.

Their efforts and 'approximations' are accepted as necessary steps to becoming confident, skilled writers. The difference is that children learn to become writers by attempting to write

• for their own purposes
• as best they are able
• in an environment, which exposes them to all that reading and writing can empower them to do.

Yes, but what about spelling?

If, when you were in school, spelling and writing were treated as separate subjects, you probably believe that spelling is efficiently learned through memorizing lists of words and that by assisting your child with weekly spelling lists you are helping him to be a better speller and writer. However, we now know children rarely transfer words learned on spelling lists to their own writing. The ability to spell is most effectively acquired through a rich exposure to reading and through genuine and persistent attempts to communicate in writing. The young child learns to write by writing and in so doing discovers the rules of written language far more effectively than through the use of workbook activities, memorizing rote spelling lists or copying from the board. The best way to help your child with spelling is the simplest and the most enjoyable: encourage reading and writing.

Just what is invented spelling?

These are the logical 'misspellings' used by children before they know the conventional or correct spelling. They are based on speech sounds and the child's knowledge of letter names and standard spelling. It is a strategy used by spellers of all ages when attempting to produce unfamiliar words

What should I say when my child asks the right way to spell words?

There's no hard and fast rule as so much depends on the situation. Always encourage independence. Grant reasonable time for the child to solve the problem for himself, but sometimes just give the help requested.

• Have the child spell as much as she can. Write the word leaving a space for each letter missed. Then together discuss and work out the rest.
• Spell it . . ..Sometimes it makes good sense simply to provide the needed information.
• If you know where the child can find the word direct him to it.

When I can't read my child's "writing", what shall I do?

• Ask, "Would you like to read it to me?"
• If there is a picture invite the child to tell you about it. Children use drawing to plan and elaborate their writing.
• Have the child read the passage while finger pointing to each word.
• Engage in a genuine discussion about the content and meaning of the child's writing.

MY Mom DokTr sd that wewr having a Moos I hrd the BaBys harel beet. It must have been really exciting to hear the baby's heart beat.

Will my child complete the work for his grade by the end of the term?

Not necessarily. Because children are unique and have different interests and experiences, they learn to read and write at their own pace Learning to walk and talk cannot be hurried, nor should learning to read and write. We must give our children the desire and confidence to learn, then provide them with experience, support and time in a print-rich, literate environment. Only they can do the rest.

What should I do when my child is frustrated?

• Acknowledge the frustration. Accept it as a normal part of learning.

• Reassurance is often all that's needed.

• Don't let your own frustration show.

• Applaud effort not just achievement.

• Provide tangible proof of progress by comparing present efforts with past writings.

• Offer to act as scribe.

• Let the child talk it through. Have her describe how she sees the problem. Listen.

Children with parents who believe in them are the children who succeed.

How can I encourage my child?

What you say to your child makes a difference Your comments signal what you value.

• Acknowledge what your child was attempting to communicate before focusing on spelling or printing. Comment on the message.

• Avoid empty words of praise. Phrases such as "That's nice", "Good work", don't really provide much information. Strive to be specific: "I love the way you described the blossoms as 'magical' in your poem."

• Don't overwhelm. One helpful suggestion is worth a dozen corrections.

• Instead of telling your child how to improve his writing, ask what he thinks would make it better.

WAYS TO FOSTER WRITING AT HOME

- Read, read, read . . . by hearing and reading stories children learn the patterns, pleasures, and power of written language.
- Encourage your child to observe the environmental print around your home; together read signs, labels , slogans, cereal boxes, junk mail . . . read EVERYTHING!
- Write notes to your child: welcome home notes, reminders, good luck wishes, riddles, happygrams, thank you notes.
- Whenever possible, involve your child when you write grocery lists, dates on calendars, messages, etc.
- Help your child keep a personal calendar of important dates and events (birthdays, library returns, hockey practice).
- Provide a writing place with plenty of paper, felts, crayons, pencils, stickers, rubber stamps.
- If possible encourage the exploration of typewriters, computers, calculators - the tools of modern writing.
- Display your child's creations with pride. Show that you value the accomplishment and effort.
- Take the lead from your child. Writing activities should build on your child's interests.
- Play games like Pictionary and Junior Scrabble
- Recognize that the stories, lists, messages and projects generated by your child are more valuable than the busy work of workbooks and coloring books. Encourage the former; avoid the latter.

POINTS TO PONDER

- The spontaneous, informal activities of daily family life provide children with many of the best opportunities for developing literacy skills. Capitalize on them.
- Time spent talking with your child about things of interest to you both contributes significantly to learning.
- Children need support and encouragement if they are to take risks and grow. Your attitude can make all the difference. Children need to know it is all right to make mistakes -- we learn from our errors.
- Each child is an individual and unique. Respect that. Enjoy it.

© A. Preece and D. Cowden, 1992.

Following the presentation and discussion, it's useful to provide parents with a handout that succinctly comments on some of the questions parents have about the beginnings of writing, describes some of the ways writing is now approached at school, and indicates how parents can support their budding writers at home (see Figure 5–5).

A copy of any handouts distributed at the meeting should be given to those parents who were unable to attend. This information also serves to inform other members of the family who might be involved in helping the child with writing, and meaningfully includes them. Reaching into the home in this manner increases the likelihood of continuity in the writing approach enacted at home and at school.

Reading a book such as *Leo the Late Bloomer* (Kraus, 1971) makes an eloquent closure to the presentation; Kraus' story poignantly expresses how all children develop in their own time and in their own ways. You might prefer to draw the session to an end by sharing a note, story or poem that is special to you, written by a child (haven't we all got some of these treasures tucked away?). Before departing, parents can be invited to suggest topics or questions they'd like addressed at future meetings; these can be recorded on a large sheet posted for the purpose, or mentioned privately to the teacher. An invitation to continue the discussion while having coffee makes a congenial ending to the evening.

Follow-Up Meetings

A sensible time to hold a second parent meeting is just prior to the first reporting period. This meeting provides an ideal opportunity to discuss any general concerns that parents might have regarding the children's writing that have arisen since the first one. Once again we strongly recommend sending home, prior to the meeting, a sheet which elicits parents' questions and queries. A follow-up meeting permits a more in-depth look at other dimensions of the writing experience (e.g. strategies to encourage editing and revising, writing for different purposes and audiences, exploring a variety of genres). Once again, writing examples taken from class work should be used to illustrate the points being discussed. If recent slides or new video footage are available of the children at work, this is an ideal time to share them. The general rule is not simply to tell about writing, but to make it possible for parents to see for themselves how children approach and manage "the orchestrated complexity" (Harste, Woodward, & Burke, 1984, p. 87) that is our writing system.

Further meetings should be held if a particular aspect of the program appears to be causing general concern. If we seriously wish to keep our parents informed and to deepen their understanding of our approach to literacy, more than a single meeting will likely be required. Although these meetings take time, time shared this way is time well and wisely invested.

Newsletters, Newspapers, and Flyers

◆

> My clas is riting
> for the noospapere
> and I am so Happy.
> This is the
> secint noos papere
> We have dun.

Newsletters are not all created equal—nor are they equally effective. The kind we're talking about here are not the P.R. sheets dutifully and regularly prepared by the school informing parents about BINGO fundraisers and the unfortunate loss by the junior boys soccer team. No, we're referring to ones that children are excited to take home and eager to share *because* they've written them themselves. When written in their own handwriting, with their own spellings retained, these newspapers become an excellent means of concretely illustrating the subtleties and complexities of children's writing.

Pointers on Publishing

In addition to keeping parents up-to-date about school events, newsletters of the type described in this book help parents understand and appreciate the acquisition and refinement of written language. There are as many formats for publishing a newspaper as the imagination can concoct. We have found two types to be particularly useful—the Flash Flyer and the Full Edition—and both are described below. The newspapers featured here were written for the parents of a first grade class, and the cover letter was designed to highlight issues relevant at that level. We've found that two or three full-edition newspapers a year, supplemented with occasional flash flyers, represent a realistic and achievable goal. It's important not to turn the publishing into a chore, nor to have the preparation of the newsletters encroach on the time available for other writing projects. As one teacher stated:

> I used your newspaper idea with a grade 3 class . . . and we were able to publish a newspaper which students were able to do from beginning to end (other than xeroxing). It was a really big hit with parents.

Flash flyers

Flash flyers are single-sheet newspapers written by the children and published intermittently. Typically, they focus on a single noteworthy event, such as announcing the hatching of incubated chicks, the visit of a pet boa constrictor, or an outbreak of chicken pox. Again, there are many possible formats; three are described below.

- *Style* 1: As a class, the children can determine and dictate the content. This is then recorded by the teacher on a sheet of paper, duplicated, and sent home. Child-created illustrations add appeal. We find this the easiest format to start with.

- *Style* 2: Together the children can generate and dictate the content, which is recorded on the board by the teacher and copied by the students. Each one then takes his or her own copy home. This model offers legitimate printing practice—the children know they are writing for a genuine audience of parents and peers. A word of caution is necessary, however. Children vary greatly with respect to printing and copying skills, and sufficient time needs to be granted in order to ensure that no child feels rushed or pressured by the task. We recommend that this format be used sparingly; the copying format can become a chore if overused. As a general rule, we feel it is more valuable for children to be engaged in generating their own writing rather than copying a model.

- *Style* 3: On a rotational basis, a group of five volunteers is given the responsibility for creating a weekly news sheet. Each child is assigned a different day and given the task of recording and illustrating what he or she considers to be the highlight of that day. All the teacher has to do is organize the contributors, provide the format, and duplicate the finished sheet. We've found it works well if blank spaces are left for Saturday and Sunday so that the children can add to their copies over the weekend (Reinhard, 1989). (See Figure 6–1.) These additions become sought-after reading material on Monday mornings.

Parents have enthusiastically responded to these flyers. They appreciate being kept in touch with the current goings-on of the classroom, especially from the children's viewpoint. As one parent commented: "We read them at the supper table, and it leads to all sorts of discussion about school. Then I send them to her grandmother—she thinks they're a hoot!"

The full-edition newspaper

Full edition newspapers contain a contribution from each child in the class (see Figure 6–2; a complete copy is included in Appendix D). Because they require more preparation than the flash flyers, usually no more than two or three "roll off the press" during the course of the year. The publication process is outlined as follows:

- Step 1: *Creating context*:
  - a) Discuss the purpose of a newspaper, using the school newsletter and/or local newspaper as examples. Familiarize children with the different sections of a paper (e.g., weather, sports, entertainment, editorials, book reviews, classified ads, lost and found, comics, crossword puzzles).

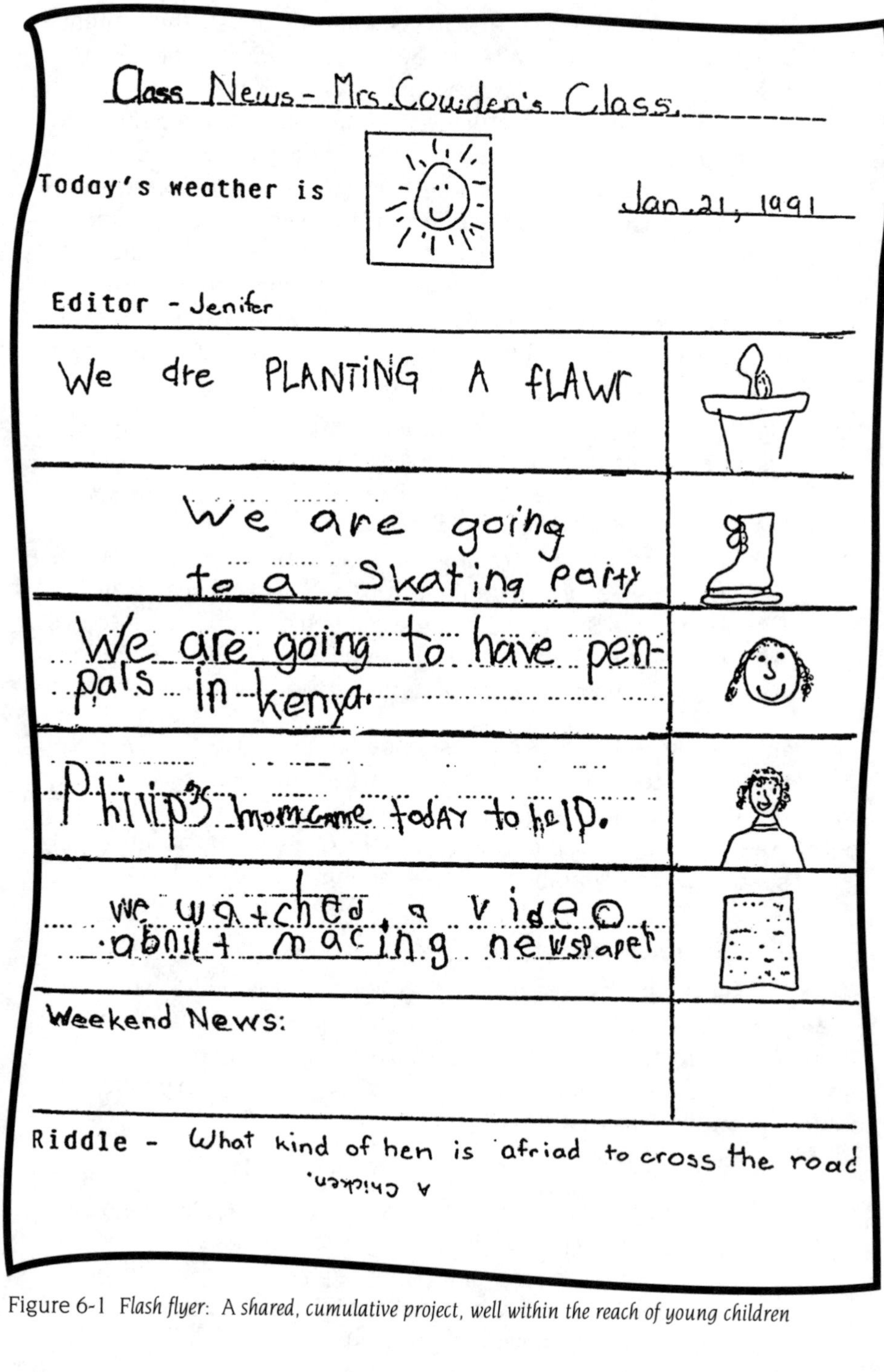

Class News - Mrs. Cowden's Class

Today's weather is ☀ Jan. 21, 1991

Editor - Jenifer

We dre PLANTING A FLAWr	
We are going to a skating party	
We are going to have pen-pals in kenya.	
Philip's mom came today to help.	
We watched a video about racing newspaper	
Weekend News:	

Riddle - What kind of hen is afriad to cross the road

A chicken.

Figure 6-1 *Flash flyer: A shared, cumulative project, well within the reach of young children*

b) If available, use a video and/or books to show how newspapers are published. This can help explain and clarify the process. Better yet is a field trip to the local newspaper office or a visit by a reporter.

- Step 2: *Creating copy: Getting ready to write*:
  a) Brainstorm with the class ideas for "articles," using the class calendars of the past few months to jog their memories. Encourage children to select newsworthy events that others will find interesting, novel, or amusing.
  b) Invite each child to choose a section to which to contribute or an idea or event to write about (e.g., one might want to write a weather report or concoct a comic strip; another might find the sports section more appealing; a third might choose to survey and report classmates' opinions of a recent field trip).
  c) Children then write draft copies of their news items. It saves time and headaches at the layout stage if the children are provided with special bordered papers of various sizes. These boxes should be sized so that they will neatly combine to fit on the newspaper page (see Figure 6–2). We recommend setting up the original layout on ledger-size paper (11" × 17") and then reducing the final copy to legal-size on the copy machine. By doing this, you grant children the space young fingers still need. An extra benefit is that the reduction process enhances the appearance of the finished product.

- Step 3: *Revisions and layout*:
  a) Final copies are written, again on the bordered sheets (the borders add a professional touch). If you or they prefer, children can write their articles on a computer; margins can easily be set to facilitate the columned format of a newspaper (see Figure 6–3).
  b) The children can be involved in all aspects of page layout, including agreeing on the paper's name (the masthead). Arrange the articles under suitable captions (created by the children). The captions can be printed by the children or designed by them on the computer. Blank spaces can be filled with illustrations related to the column topic.

- Step 4: *Putting the paper to bed*:
  a) The newspaper sheets are reduced in size on the copier and duplicated.
  b) A cover letter from the teacher (discussed on pp. 74–75) is attached, and the newspapers are distributed to the children to take home.

Figure 6-2 Fall *newspaper*

OUR NEWSPAPER

Pablishd by al the kids in Mrs. Cowden's clas

MOMS AND DADS

Chris' dad came to talk about forests. He came on anti-litter week and he wrks for the minustar of invermnt.

Chris

Tommarow night is fun night. Elizabeth's mom is helping.

Julie and Elizabeth

On Monday Lindsay's mom came and tot as jym. Lindsay's mom hallpt us on the box Lindsay's mom did sum warm ups with music.

Moms come in to help the clas room theyh holp us to red and cract our riting. I like them cuming in.

Joey

Flash

Jennifer's mom had a baby girl on May 31. Her name is

Megan Briane   By Jennifer

Figure 6-3 *Newspaper done on computer*

One issue we've wrestled with and continue to debate is whether or not to identify the contributions of each child by attaching names to the "articles." Obviously the concern is to avoid having parents compare the achievements of specific children. On the other hand, children take great pride in seeing their work identified as their own. We have tried it both ways—with the names and without them. Without a doubt, the children prefer to have their names appear. When a group of our parents were specifically asked to state a preference, however, many opted to have the names left off. One solution may be to give each child the option of an identified or anonymous contribution; it then becomes a personal rather than group decision. This is one issue you might want to talk over with your parents at the first meeting.

Some teachers have expressed concern about possible parental reactions to the great variation in writing competence revealed when the different articles in the newspaper are compared. For instance, it's not unusual to find in a first-grade edition a piece written by a child who is still representing whole words with a single wobbly letter next to the work of another who is well on the way to mastery of conventional spelling. The fear is that some parents will interpret these differences as indicative of deficiencies on the part of their child and worry that their child is "behind." It's wise to raise this issue during the parent meetings. It's very important that parents be made aware that a wide range of competence is *the norm*, and that it is inevitable and expected that different children in the class will be at different points on the continuum of writing competence. The differences reflect the nature of literacy acquisition and the fact that individuals learn according to their own unique schedules. It's also useful to point out that in any one class children will differ in age by up to twelve months (more, in some groupings), to say nothing of differences in experience and interest. The important thing is to assure parents that each child is provided with multiple opportunities to explore written language, and that each is making sense of those experiences in a way that is personally relevant and appropriate. Differences are normal, natural, necessary—and our instructional practices are now finally beginning to honor them.

These newspapers are in two parts: a child-written portion and a cover letter written by the teacher. The point of the letter is to highlight and help explain (and sometimes interpret) the development of writing as evident in the children's articles. The information presented should be accessible but not overly simplified or generalized. By drawing parents' attention to specific examples in the newspaper, the teacher is able to offer concrete illustrations of the strategies children employ as they learn to write. Obviously, the content of the cover letter is dependent on the nature of the children's writing samples. The cover letter in Figure 6–4 was sent to parents of six- and seven-year-olds; should you be working with older children, the focus of the letter would be adjusted accordingly. Similarly, if you publish two or three newspapers during the year, the content and focus of the accompanying letters will shift to reflect the progress made and the understandings and insights being acquired by the children.

It is important that the covering letters reinforce points made during the parent meetings. We've found that one effective way to organize these letters is to divide them into three short sections. The first points to specifics of writing development exemplified by the children's newspaper articles. The next section addresses questions and concerns that parents have raised or provides background information about a particular aspect of writing. The third section suggests some ways that parents can support and enrich their child's learning. Reminders about upcoming events, speakers, or books available for borrowing also can be featured. Length and density of content should be adjusted to make the letter appropriate for your parent group. As in all communications with parents, tone is all-important. The goal is to share information while avoiding prescription, preaching, or pressure. The lengthy cover letter in Figure 6–4 was written in the early spring to accompany the second newspaper published by a first-grade class (a complete copy of this newspaper can be found in Appendix D).

It is advisable for the principal to have an opportunity to read the newspaper before it goes home. This prevents any misunderstandings and keeps him or her informed both about children's writing and the goings-on in your classroom.

A word of caution: As much as parents may welcome the newsletter and other aspects of a parent-participation program, they might not always openly express their appreciation. Experience has taught us, however, it is unwise to assume that because little feedback is volunteered the effort is not valued. Parents who have never mentioned the newsletter, for example, have shown their endorsement by specifically requesting that younger siblings be placed in classrooms where similar efforts are made to keep parents informed and where children's initial attempts at writing are respected. Our formal surveys of the parents have unquestionably established that the newsletters provide insight and information about the writing process that significantly helps them to understand some of the

May, 1992

Dear Parents,

I'm delighted to once again share the children's writing with you. They've really worked hard to put this newspaper together and are justly proud of their efforts. I'm sure you'll be as impressed as I am with the confidence, creativity, and growing competence displayed by these young writers.

As you read the children's news items, I hope you find the following comments and observations helpful.

Content and Attitude:
• The children are freely taking risks and experimenting with their writing. Writing vocabularies are expanding, and most children are willing to tackle almost any word, whether they know the conventional spelling or not ("inchrasted" = interested; "hyacnths" = hyacinths).
• The language encountered in the books they're reading is being incorporated into their writings ("One day a little robin was flying. . .").
• Sensitivity to tone, style, and voice is increasingly evident ("Noo to the weather rept with Philip Splle..."; note how Philip has captured "weatherese").
• Selections are lengthier and feelings and emotions are being portrayed ("juming and spe nening and moving ther legs and smieling and smiling").
• Most important of all, a positive attitude toward writing is evident ("I gast get inchrasted in riting about cats"; "A lot of peppl do rit a lot . . We like to rit").

Spelling:
• Gradually, vowel sounds are becoming more accurately represented and now are rarely omitted ("mamith" = mammoth)
• Vowel combinations are being explored ("copooder" = computer; "owr"= our; "peepull" = people; "eech" = each).
• Beginning, ending, and middle sounds now are consistently represented ("moozeyom" = museum; "dansis" = dances).
• The letter-name strategy still is relied on to create long vowel sounds ("grad" = grade; "rit" = write; "paj" = page).
• Plural "s" and "-ing" endings are consistently used ("tching" = teaching; "riting" = writing; "dinosors" = dinosaurs).

Printing:
• Printing is more legible; fine motor control gains are apparent; letter size is shrinking.

Figure 6-4 A note, similar to this one, can help alleviate parent's concerns

• For the most part, upper- and lowercase letters are used appropriately.
• Words are separated and spaced, and some children now can handle letter placement on lined paper.
• Punctuation is beginning to appear, although it's almost entirely limited to the use of periods and exclamation marks. Some children are exploring the use of apostrophes ("baskit's" = baskets).

You were asking about . . . A number of people have asked me why children sometimes write two or three different versions of the same word within the same piece of work (e.g., "smieling and smiling"), or represent the same sound in a variety of different ways, sometimes within the same sentence (e.g., "mayd"; "mad"; "made"). This is rarely a sign of carelessness, but indicates instead how closely children attend to the construction of each and every word. For example, "smieling" and "smiling" both accurately track the sound of the word; the difference in the spellings is likely a result of the child stressing and elongating the vowel differently when sounding it out, and then recording the sounds actually heard. Often, the use of different spellings for the same word reflects children's awareness of the fact that the same sound can be represented in a variety of ways. By creating different versions of the word or sound, the child reveals his/her awareness of the options available. What he or she is not yet certain of is which option is the conventional, or correct, one.

Supporting your young writer at home . . . One of the very best ways we can help children become better writers is to continue to read to them. Reading, and being read to, extends and enriches the resources a child can bring to writing in a multitude of ways. Regular exposure to good books (fiction and nonfiction) familiarizes children with the structures and patterns of written language, with vocabulary they might not otherwise encounter, and with stylistic devices that heighten impact and effect. The bedtime story remains one of the most powerful and pleasurable ways yet discovered to boost children into literacy. So . . . continue to squeeze that reading in!

Our parent library has acquired a new book you may find interesting: <u>Literacy Begins at Birth,</u> by Marjorie Fields. Marvellously readable, it's full of information and suggestions. Drop in, or send a note, if you'd like to borrow it.

Once again, thanks for all your support. It makes such a difference.

intricacies of their child's growth as a writer. When asked to rate the value of the newsletters, one group of parents stated that they would not have been able to appreciate or accept the teacher's approach to writing without them. The majority claimed that the newsletters had helped change their ideas of how writing is learned, and thus of how it should be taught. A sampling of their comments follow:

It points out the progress not necessarily obvious.

I love the newsletters—and I've saved them all. Tony reads them to his Dad and his baby-sitter . . . I've learned so much from them.

When I helped him at home, I would have resorted to the old ways I was taught if it hadn't been for all the meetings and things you gave us.

SEVEN

Writing Projects that Link Home and School

—— • ◆ • ——

"What writers need is time, ownership, reasons to care, responsive readers, and shoulders upon which to stand." L.M. CALKINS, 1990

There are all sorts of imaginative ways to encourage the free flow of children's writing between home and school. One indicator that your efforts to encourage writing are succeeding comes from finding that the writing activities of the classroom spill over into the home. By the same token, one way to foster writing production outside the classroom is to grant children an audience at school for the writing they've created at home. If encouraged, children will bring in all manner of "literacy artifacts." Much of this will occur spontaneously. Sometimes, however, special projects such as those described in the following section work wonderfully to initiate this two-way exchange.

Puppet News

One writing activity that has proven unfailingly popular and appealing involves "home visits" by a set of classroom puppets. Taking turns, each child is given the opportunity to take one of the puppets home overnight. Three or four puppets are sufficient for this project, and the plush animal variety have proven to have the most appeal for the young children we have worked with. While at home, each child is asked to write a short note, which we call the puppet news, reporting on the events experienced by the puppet during the visit. The puppets' adventures have ranged from having peas for supper to being invited to a sleepover to riding in a helicopter. On the puppet's return, this note is read to the class by its author (with or without assistance). Questions from classmates are then invited and answered. This sharing provides the child with an interested audience and a genuine reason for writing the note. The note is then posted on a special section of the bulletin board so that others may read it if they wish. Eventually these notes are dated and placed in the children's portfolios.

The point and purpose of the puppet news (see Figure 7–1 for an example) needs to be explained at a parents' meeting before the puppet visits begin. It is important to clarify your expectations with respect to the parents' role. Stress that the writing is to be done by the child—as much as is possible—but that parents should feel free to assist when help is sought. The following suggestions may provide parents with some guidelines for helping their child write these puppet notes.

- Respond to the meaning and the message before commenting on the mechanics.
- Accept the child's spelling and printing approximations. Gradually they will be replaced with standard spellings, although functional spelling will still be used for unfamiliar words.
- If you feel the need to suggest changes or corrections, limit these to one or two and offer them only if your child is receptive.
- If your child is frustrated or tired, act as scribe.
- As the child becomes a more fluent and skilled writer, encourage the elaboration of a single event rather than the stringing together of a series of incidents.

The purpose of the travelling puppets is to encourage written communication, and the task is deliberately open-ended so that each child can bring to it the knowledge and resources he or she has available. Helping the child with the note gives parents the opportunity to observe and encourage their child's efforts to write and serves to reinforce and deepen understanding of the information presented during the parent meetings and in the newsletters. The puppet notes will vary considerably; some will be completely scribed by parents, some will be decipherable only by the child, and some will intermingle functional and conventional spellings. The form of these notes can provide the teacher with a great deal of information about the type of assistance provided for the children. For example, if a child's invented spellings have been scrupulously corrected, then it is fair to assume that whoever worked with that child is not yet comfortable with (or familiar with, or accepting of) the philosophy you have been attempting to communicate.

Helpfuls Lournal Brooke.
Feduany 4
When School Was over
me anb Helpful Bent a Kaek

for ASHlY it is a Towlit Kaek
We Wil Play gems

Figure 7-1 Puppet News *written by Brooke, age 6*

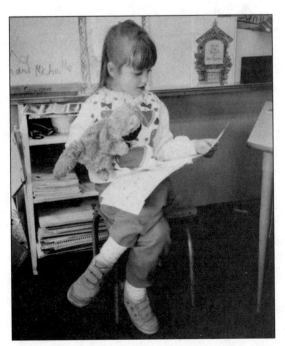

Puppets make the presentations easier—the child is not alone.

Pride is visible when the note is pinned up for everyone to see.

The children eagerly anticipate their turn to take home a puppet and are quick to remind forgetful peers about late returns. One year a lost puppet resulted in child-written signs and reward notices being posted all around the school. A rotational schedule needs to be worked out to organize the turns. If a list of names is posted the turns can be easily monitored and managed by the children themselves. The first time each student takes home a puppet, it's helpful if a note similar to the one in Figure 7–2 accompanies it.

The puppet project is easily managed if you:

- Give children the responsibility of keeping track of whose turn it is to take the puppets home.

Bo Bear's Visit

My name is Bo Bear and I am so happy that I am coming home with you. Please help me write a note about my visit. We can read together to our friends when we go back to school tomorrow. Please take good care of me.

   Thank you,

Bo Bear

P.S It's okay to ask a grown-up to help you with the writing you need to.

Figure 7-2 *An accompanying note lets parents know what is expected*

- Stress to the children the importance of bringing the puppet back to school each day. After a few warnings, losing the privilege of taking the puppet home the next time usually eliminates this problem.
- Have the children choose their own paper for writing the news rather than having a blank booklet accompany the puppet. Such books have a way of going astray. More importantly, letting the children supply their own paper sidesteps the possibility that parents will feel subtle pressure to have their child maintain the standard set by previous entries.

Plastic or cloth bags need to be provided to transport the puppets between home and school. We've found that puppets cared for in this manner do not need to be replaced for at least three to four years. Even if they do become somewhat shopworn, the children become so attached to the puppets that appearance becomes unimportant.

Brothers and sisters coming into the class and children in multiage classes who remain with the same teacher for several years will make sure the tradition of the puppet news is carried on. After experiencing the puppet visits throughout the school year, one parent remarked: "The puppet coming home made all the difference to my child adjusting to school and it gave me a reason to sit and talk with him about his writing. . . . I have a soft spot for that puppet."

An Ounce of Prevention:
Sending Journals and Writing Books Home

The first time written work using functional spelling is sent home it can cause genuine concern for parents when they find few corrections and what appear to them as bizarre spelling errors. A note (see Figure 7–3) glued into the front cover of the child's journal or writing book can help alleviate this concern. Parents who were not present at any of the informational meetings about young children's writing would especially benefit from such an explanation.

Some teachers use a variation of the daily journal, sometimes referred to as home-school journals, to keep communication flowing between the classroom and the home. These are set up in much the same fashion as dialogue journals and are prefaced with a note explaining the procedure (see Figure 7–4 for an example). The child writes an entry on a topic of his or her choice and then takes the journal home where the entry is read to and/or by the parent or another member of the family, who then responds to the child in writing. Sometimes the teacher adds comments or questions for the parent(s) or write a response to the child's or parents' entries. Self-sealing plastic bags work well to protect the journals (usually conventional school exercise books) while they're in transit. Home-school journals work well with students of all ages. With young children they work best if sent home on a weekly basis. Fridays are recommended as take-home days, as that grants the parents the full weekend in which to respond. These journals tend to turn into treasures that are kept.

All in Good Time

As you read through your child's writings you may wonder why I have not corrected the errors that are so evident. Let me assure you, I have good reasons for exercising red pencil restraint. In writing their journals the children are encouraged to express their personal thoughts about experiences important to them. In my conferences with them, I respond first to the content and then invite the students to talk about any problems they've encountered with their writing. By emphasizing meaning before mechanics, the real purpose of writing as a means of communication is made clear. Children of this age find constant correction of every mistake overwhelming and defeating. My goal is to help create confident, skilled writers. To accomplish this they must be given freedom to experiment and explore writing on their own terms.

For children to grow as writers they need to have:
• the support of an attentive adult who follows their lead and responds to the meaning of their writings,
• many opportunities to express themselves in writing,
• their approximations accepted and their efforts acknowledged,
• the opportunity to write for an audience, and
• the satisfaction and pride of occasionally producing an edited copy.

Thank you for taking the time to show your appreciation and to give your encouragement and praise to your budding author.

_____
(Teacher)

Figure 7-3 *Parents can worry when they find few corrections to their child's writing*

Dear Parents,

　　The children will be bringing home their home-school journals every Friday to share their news with you and other family members. The journals need to be returned on Mondays. I know you will enjoy reading what has been written. When time permits, please reply to your child on the next page. Responses from brothers and sisters also are welcome. These messages can come to mean a great deal.

　　Thank you for supporting your child's writing in this way.

　　　　　　　　　　　　　　　———————————————
　　　　　　　　　　　　　　　　(teacher's signature)

Figure 7-4 *Letter prefacing home-school journals (Adapted from a model by Muriel Hemmes, McKinney Elementary School, Richmond, B.C.)*

Personal Calendars for Home and Classroom Use

Calendars are ideal vehicles for encouraging planning and for modeling another real-life use of writing. One way to capitalize on them is to provide each child with two personal copies of a blank September-to-September calendar, with a sheet for each month and large boxes for each day. One calendar is kept at school and the other taken home. The children can be encouraged to record dates and events that have significance for them (family birthdays, visits to grandparents, team games and practices, first lost tooth). Parents enjoy assisting their children with this activity and find it helps the children to remember when to bring back library books, which are the gym days, etc. A larger version can be made to

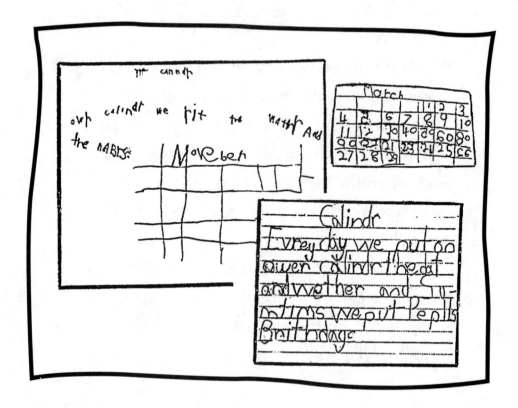

serve the entire class; during the first week of school children can work in pairs to illustrate the class calendar, with each pair given the responsibility for one monthly sheet. As a special project, calendars can be illustrated by different groups of children; these then can be duplicated and used as a fundraiser or given away as gifts.

Special Events Booklets and Anthologies

There are many special occasions that occur throughout the year that can be turned into writing opportunities (e.g., Earth Day, Grandparents' Appreciation Day, Valentines, and Thanksgiving). For example, to mark Mothers' Day, the children can be asked to write a special letter to Mom (or to an interested adult of their choice—we acknowledge the sensitivity and care that needs to be exercised when dealing with issues of family). These are then illustrated, collected (with the children's permission), mounted in a class booklet, duplicated, and presented as a gift. A Junior Gourmet Booklet that features descriptions of each child's favorite meal

Calendars become a record, a reference, and a resource when children are allowed to become active participants in their creation.

can be a delightful and humorous project. If Mothers' or Fathers' Day is the topic selected, we recommend you encourage the children to think about what their parents mean to them or *do* for and with them rather than focus on things they buy for them. If unedited by the teacher, the samples provide parents with examples of the range of writing competence demonstrated by children of this age level. They also give the children a genuine writing activity—and a guaranteed appreciative audience. On occasion, you might want to emphasize presentation. In the samples featured in Figure 7–5, the children were encouraged (and helped) to "make a good copy," focusing on the appearance of their printing and standard spelling.

Insistence upon a copy corrected to adult standard should be weighed carefully. Sometimes it will be appropriate and sometimes not. An end-of-the-
year anthology featuring a selection of writing samples from each student
makes a treasured souvenir for both parent and child. Extra copies should
be available for other family members or friends who may request one.

Figure 7-5 *Projects such as this Mother's Day booklet become treasured mementoes*

EIGHT

Evaluation Is Made More Meaningful

◆

"Like reading, writing develops over many years, with both common patterns in development and individual differences in timing and ways of learning." BRITISH COLUMBIA MINISTRY OF EDUCATION, *Supporting Learning*, 1991

Parents who have attended the information meetings, read the newsletters, and observed or assisted in the classroom generally have a distinct advantage when it comes to understanding and interpreting the evaluations and comments on their children's report cards. At the very least, they will have some familiarity with the instructional context and some insight into the range of competence typically displayed by children who are approximately the same age as their own. They also are more likely to be aware of the criteria, values, and emphases that undergird your evaluations of the children's writings. Put differently, they will have some sense of what it is that you look for when assessing the writing produced by their child.

Because so much has changed in the way teachers approach and undertake evaluation, it's a good idea to spend some time during the information meetings describing how you monitor and assess the children's growth as writers. It is important to clearly communicate the importance of monitoring *attitude* (the way children feel about writing; whether they initiate or avoid writing opportunities; whether they view themselves as writers), *approach* and *strategies used* (how a child prepares for, and executes, a writing task; whether the child is a risk taker and experimenter; whether the child prefers to work independently or collaboratively), and the *resourcefulness* displayed (how problems are tackled; whether the child knows where and how to obtain help or information), as well as the insights and understandings about writing that are revealed in the child's products. In the past, the evaluative focus was firmly on the correctness (or lack of it) of the children's written *products*, and, in the primary grades, the mechanics of printing and spelling tended to receive more attention than the content, or quality of the ideas being expressed. Now, in addition to attending to the mechanics (which are important), teachers first focus on the ideas and meanings being communicated and the nature of each child's experience of the *process* of writing.

Parents need to be informed of this shift and also given an indication of how you keep track of your students' learning and growth. This can be easily handled during the information meetings if you show them a child's portfolio or writing folder and explain how dated samples are periodically selected, analyzed, and kept to provide a record of what each child has accomplished. If you document their writing in a conference log or record book, it's useful to mention this and to explain the sort of observations that would be recorded. Similarly, if you encourage the children to self-evaluate, it can be both informative and instructive for parents to hear the type of questions you ask of children to encourage them to be analytical and reflective about their writing. Parents are often surprised, and impressed, when they become aware of the care routinely taken by good teachers to evaluate and record the learning of each child in their classes. It's then not as difficult to convince them that the descriptive richness of the information available to them from the portfolio and the teacher's anecdotal record is of far more value than a single grade or numerical score.

Those parents who accept the invitations to observe or participate in the classroom will be in a better position to appreciate—and see for themselves—how evaluation can be a positive, ongoing, and integral part of the learning activities, and how much can be learned by observing and attending to the daily work produced by the children. By the same token, teachers can take advantage of the opportunities provided by a parent's presence in the classroom to discover more about his or her child. Parents are key informants about their own children, and, if invited, they can provide invaluable information about their children's learning, attitudes, and reactions to the classroom. Invitations need be no more complicated than a simple inquiry. A brief letter asking parents to note their observations and impressions of their child as a learner, reader, or writer can generate a gold mine of information. Parents appreciate being asked and interpret the inquiry as evidence that their knowledge of their children is recognized and valued. Choosing not to tap this source of information is choosing to teach with one hand tied behind your back.

When parents are aware of the attitudes, strategies, and understandings that are being cultivated in your classroom, it's easier for them to support your efforts by reinforcing them at home. Over 80 percent of the more than twelve hundred parents surveyed by Epstein (1986) reported a willingness to work more closely with their child's teacher, but indicated a desire for some guidance as to how to go about it. Children are less likely to be caught between two contradictory orientations to education in general, and writing in particular, if teachers and parents have an opportunity to discuss the criteria each considers important.

Parent-teacher reporting conferences are the customary vehicle for keeping parents informed about their child's learning and progress. These, too, can be very different from the ones parents remember from their own school days. For one thing, it's now common practice for children to be invited to attend along with their parents. For another, in an attempt

to ensure the conferences are relevant and focused, parents are more and more often being asked, prior to the scheduled date, to indicate which areas they particularly wish to have addressed during the meeting (Anthony, Johnson, Mickelson, Preece, 1991). Also, rather than being regarded as a time simply to report on the progress or gains noted over the previous term, the conference time is increasingly being used to establish and negotiate goals and priorities for the next few months of school. All are changes we heartily endorse.

Parent-teacher conferences offer an ideal opportunity to refer to and update any goal sheets that were filled in earlier in the year (see page 36) and to determine ways that parents can work with you to continue to support their child's learning. This mutual focus on significant goals signals a personalized and responsive stance toward evaluation. The goal focus also provides a constructive, forward-looking context for dealing with any problems the child might be having. Parents usually are very clear about their desire to be informed promptly about any problems or learning difficulties experienced by their child. A strength of the goal sheet is that it makes devising a plan of action easier, and it's structured so that *both* the parents and the teacher are involved in implementing it.

The contents of the child's writing folder can be shared during the conference and specific examples highlighted to illustrate and support the comments made on the report. If the children attend the conferences, they can be invited to point out any accomplishments *they* feel are worth noting. This can easily be structured by giving them the opportunity to choose a writing sample they regard as being one of their best and having them explain to their parents their reasons for feeling so. Evaluation serves learners well when it makes them aware of their strengths rather than simply pointing to areas in need of attention.

Parent involvement in education has powerful and positive implications for evaluation. When parents, teachers, and students work together in a spirit of openness, reciprocity, and mutual respect, everybody gains.

NINE

Understanding Leads to Change

❖

"Strategies to involve parents represent one of the most powerful underutilized instruments for educational reform." FULLAN, 1991

Efforts to involve and include parents in the learning and school experiences of their children can have obvious and lasting benefits for both parents and students. Sometimes unrecognized, however, are the rewards for teachers. One is certainly the regard, respect, and affection that parents so often feel for those teachers who "invite them in." Sometimes this isn't expressed directly, however, and teachers are left unaware of the impact of all their hard work. There's no doubt that efforts to involve parents make a difference. As Epstein (1986) reports:

> Parents with children in the classrooms of teachers who built parent involvement into their regular teaching practice were more aware of teachers' efforts, received more ideas from teachers, knew more about their child's instructional program, and rated the teachers higher in interpersonal skills and overall teaching quality. (p. 291)

Efforts to include parents *are* noticed, and valued—and their impact is powerful and far-reaching. For all sorts of reasons, we need to reach beyond the concept of the home-school relationship we have known in the past to create and build meaningful parent-teacher-student dialogues and alliances. They matter, and they make a difference.

As we sifted and sorted through the piles of children's writing that we've both accumulated over the years, looking for examples to include in our book, we found ourselves once again impressed, intrigued, and moved by the intelligence, resourcefulness, and sensitivity of young children. Perhaps, after all is said and done, the most important thing we can do for the parents of our students is to help them see their children's writing as we do . . . so they can be as amazed, impressed, and humbled by it —*by them*— as we are.

"The responsibility is ours. The future is theirs." (Doake, 1988).

A Parent Library

◆

The following books are recommended because they have been particularly well received by parents. Additional suggestions can be found in Jane Baskwill's book *Parents and Teachers—Partners in Learning* and Regie Routman's book *Transitions: From Literature to Literacy*. The International Reading Association has booklets and pamphlets available for parents at modest cost. Starting a parent library from scratch can be an expensive proposition for a school, but it's possible to start small and build the collection over the years. Parents are often more than willing to raise funds for this worthwhile project or allocate a portion of their school association budget for it. Such contributions should be acknowledged by placing Donor Recognition Labels (see Figure A–1) inside the front covers.

Figure A-1 *Donor Recognition labels*

The form shown in Figure A–2 could be adapted to facilitate book borrowing from the parent library. The request form with accompanying annotations works well to generate interest in the books available. It's best to send the books home in clear self-sealing plastic bags that are labelled

---

Would you like to . . .

BORROW A BOOK?

The books listed below are for you and your family to share and enjoy. An annotated bibliography of each book is attached to provide you with additional information. You may sign out a book of your choice for a two week period.

`--------------------- (tear) ---------------------------`

I would be interested in having the following book(s):

	Choice	
	1st	*2nd*
Literacy Begins at Birth (Fields, M,V. 1989)		
Writing Begins at Home (Clay, M. 1987)		
What Did I Write? (Clay, M. 1975)		
Craft of Children's Writing (Newman, J. 1984)		
Spel . . . is a Four-Letter Word (Gentry, J.R. 1987)		
What's Whole in Whole Language? (Goodman, K. 1986)		
Kids Have All the Write Stuff (Edwards & Maloy, 1992)		
Luk Mume Luk Dade I Kan Rit (Villiers, U. 1989)		
A Guide to Childrens' Spelling Development (Tarasoff, M. 1992)		
Reading Begins at Home (Clay, M. & Butler, D. 1982)		
Landsberg's Guide to Chldren's Books (Landsberg, M. 1986)		
The New Read-Aloud Handbook (Trelease, J. 1989)		
MegaSkills (Rich, D. 1988)		
Love Dad (Connolly, P. 1985)		

Name _____   Phone _____

If you are interested in having any of these books for a two week period please indicate above which ones you would like and return this form by _____.

Figure A-2 *Advertising the books increases their circulation*

(computer address labels work well) with the school's and teacher's name clearly marked. Parents' committees are sometimes willing to make a project of sewing sturdy, attractive canvas or nylon bags for the Parent Library, and these can certainly add pizzazz and attract notice.

As an extra bonus, you might consider tucking a book for the child into the bag. If judiciously chosen, the books can complement each other and potentially serve to deepen the parent's appreciation of the book they had asked to borrow. For example, a possible pairing could be Judith Newman's *The Craft of Children's Writing* with *The Jolly Postman, or Other People's Letters*, by the Ahlbergs.

Suggested Books About Writing for the Parent Library

Butler, D. & Clay, M. 1982. *Reading Begins at Home: Preparing Children for Reading Before They Go To School*. Portsmouth, NH: Heinemann.
> The authors answer many of the questions parents have about how best to introduce young children into reading. Reassuring and respectful, the book validates parents' role as significant supporters of their child's literacy, suggests activities, and explains some of the instructional methods in place in our schools. Slim—and powerful.

Clay, M. 1975. *What Did I Write* ? Portsmouth, NH: Heinemann.
> This brief but excellent book explains the importance of allowing children to be self-directing in their early writings. The relevance of early reading to writing is also discussed.

Clay, M. 1987. *Writing Begins at Home: Preparing Children For Writing Before They Go To School*. Portsmouth, NH: Heinemann.
> Written for the parents of preschoolers, this slim, colorful volume contains a rich demonstration of the insights and understandings young children acquire as they explore and experiment with written language. Clay helps parents see for themselves the intelligent and inventive ways that children gradually gain command over print. Questions commonly asked by parents are answered in a straightforward manner, and guidance is given for ways of supporting children's moves towards literacy. Inviting, informing, and not overwhelming.

Connolly, P. 1985. *Love, Dad: A Father's Daily Epistles to His Two Boys. Written on the Run and Left on the Breakfast Table*. Kansas City, NY: Andrew, McMeel & Parker.
> Parents will be moved by this book, which models the power of note writing to one's children.

Edwards, S.A., & Maloy, R.W. 1992. *Kids Have All the Write Stuff: Inspiring Your Children to Put Pencil to Paper.* New York, NY: Penguin.

Written for parents, the book offers an inviting blend of current information about how writing is learned with a multitude of appealing and realistic suggestions for ways parents can encourage, support, and enrich their children's explorations of written language. Designed to foster initiative, risk taking, autonomy, and confidence, the recommended activities are refreshingly child-centered and engaging. Informative, accessible, and theoretically grounded, the book is full of practical advice that respects the creativity and capabilities of both parents and children. The authors include an excellent section on using computers with children and also provide a comprehensive survey of recommended materials and resources. No parent library should be without a copy of this book.

Fields, M.V. 1989. *Literacy Begins at Birth.* Tucson, AZ: Fisher Books.

A book that parents will enjoy reading that explains how children from birth through age seven learn to read and write using an integrated literacy approach. Field describes the role of parents in this process and details what to look for in a supportive school environment.

Gentry, J.R. 1987. *Spel. . . Is a Four-Letter Word.* Portsmouth, NH: Heinemann.

In this concise, easy-to-read handbook the inadequacies of memorized weekly spelling lists are compared to a more practical and appropriate approach—that of encouraging invented spelling. Gentry answers questions frequently asked about spelling. In the words of one parent, "It helped me understand the stages a child goes through in learning to spell."

Goodman, K. 1986. *What's Whole in Whole Language.* Portsmouth, NH: Heinemann.

Although written for teachers, this is a useful book for parents who want to know about whole language. It dispels the fear that whole language is just a passing fashion. Goodman offers a clearly written summary of the key characteristics of this philosophy. An excellent book to use at parents' meetings.

Landsberg, M. 1986. *Landsberg's Guide to Children's Books.* Markham, Ont: Penguin.

Parents who wish to pass on to their children a rich heritage of children's literature will find this reference book invaluable.

Newman, J. 1984. *The Craft of Children's Writing*. Richmond Hill, Ont.: Scholastic-TAB Publications.

> A book that clearly explains to parents the writing development of children. Deservedly popular.

Rich, D. 1988: *Megaskills; How families can help children succeed in school and beyond*. Boston, MA: Houghton Mifflin.

> Included in this book are a multitude of suggestions for ways parents can involve their children in enriching homework activities.

Trelease, J. 1989. *The New Read-Aloud Handbook*. New York: Penguin.

> With infectious enthusiasm, Trelease advocates reading aloud to children of all ages and argues persuasively for the value of making book-sharing a regular event both at home and at school. An annotated bibliography of recommended read-alouds, categorized by type, provides ready access to a wealth of fine literature. His discussion of the impact of television shouldn't be missed.

Villiers, U. 1989. LUK MUME LUK DADE I KAN RIT. Richmond Hill Ont.: Scholastic-TAB Publications.

> A book beautifully illustrated with the writing produced by a group of young inner-city children. Warm, insightful, and informing, this makes a marvellous follow-up to a presentation on children's writing.

Time -Line Depiction

◆

One Child's Growth as a Writer Between the Ages of Three and Eight Years

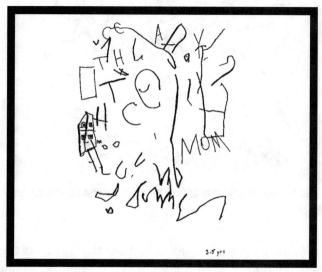

(3.5 years)

- Children often curious about letters and print will ask, "What does this say?"
- Parents associate how their children, as infants, strung sounds together with the intonation of an adult's speech with how children string letters together so they have the appearance of adult writing.
- All the letters of her name are present, although not in linear sequence.
- Upper case letters are favored.
- Letter-like strings appear; child knows what writing looks like and clearly distinguishes it from her drawings.
- MOM is a sight word, likely copied; note this is a personally meaningful word—children want to represent and write about things that matter to them.

(4 *years*)

- As they learn to speak, children sort out the sounds of their mother tongue. Similarly, as they learn to write, children distinguish significant differences in the symbol system.

- Name is now written in correct sequence and set off clearly as a separate word.

- Plays with letter-like strokes—imitating writing.

- Child aware of top-to-bottom, left-to-right page orientation.

- Uppercase letters still prefered.

- *Possible* attempt to write numbers and to distinguish them from letters.

- Pretend writing continues (series of circles with internal dots); note that child now aware that writing is built from combinations of separate letters.

(4.6 years)

- Words featured are important to the child; *meaning matters*.
- A *beginning* awareness of word boundaries (e.g., her name is separated, but the other words are run together).
- Child is likely copying and/or working from memory.
- N is reversed—this provides an opportunity to comment on reversals and to reassure parents that they do not usually signal a visual or learning problem.
- Uppercase letters still prefered.

(5.10 years)

- First appearance of a phrase.
- Child is clearly using writing to convey a message.
- First appearance of invented or constructive spelling, used in combination with copied/sight words.
- The word "you" is represented by the letter "U"; note how child uses letter *name* to convey sound wanted.
- Lowercase letters are now appearing, mixed with uppercase.
- Word boundaries clearly established.
- Revision and/or self-correction is evident; note scribbled out phrase.
- Heightened awareness of detail in letter formation is paralleled by a similar emphasis on detail in her drawings.
- Drawing illustrates the written message.

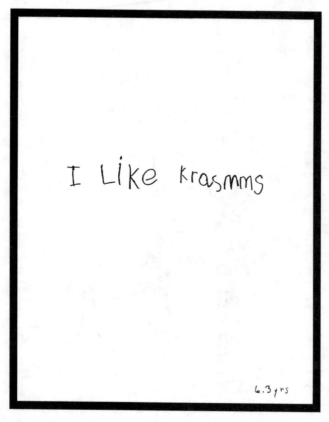

I Like krasmms

6.3 yrs

(6.3 years)

- When uttering their first words children leave out many of the sounds, just as they do when they begin to write sound-symbol relationships.

- Constructive spelling used for word beyond her spelling vocabulary ("krasmms" for "Christmas"); note how closely the child is attending to the sounds actually heard.

- Vowel and consonant sounds are differentiated ("krasmms"); child is becoming aware of need to represent obvious vowel sounds.

- The vowel used is the vowel found in the child's name (Cathy); this is a common strategy used by the emergent writer.

- No punctuation evident.

(6.4 *years*)

- Complete sentence with punctuation.
- Letter-name strategy still employed ("k<u>u</u>t" for "cute").
- More lowercase letters appearing, randomly mixed with uppercase.
- Beginning awareness of vowel combinations ("Thae").
- Increasing experimentation with vowels, yet sound-letter match still unconventional.
- The *n* sound in "thank" is not represented ("thak") because it is difficult to distinguish and it isn't felt in the mouth when the child articulates the word.
- Child's response to adult's written comment demonstrates child's understanding of function of writing.

me AND mi
Buddy Are
Letting mi
Balloon go
Too day
.P.S. I hop
mi Balloon
doesn't Pop
6.5 yrs

(6.5 years)

- Child is incorporating words from books and reference charts ("balloon"; "doesn't").

- Selections are noticeably longer.

- Even though much more competence evident in the representation of vowel sounds, letter-name strategy still relied upon ("mi" for "my"; "hop" for "hope").

- Aware of varied ways of spelling "to" ("too").

- Post-script abbreviation used (P.S.); note overgeneralization of period here, and its absence at end of sentence.

- As in each previous example, child writes about things of personal interest and significance.

(6.8 years)

- Child explores a different genre: songwriting.
- Song has a title, which is set apart.
- Child exploits and adapts a familiar model ("I can sing a rainbow").
- Upper- and lowercase letters now used appropriately.
- Child attempts to convey the elongation of the vowel sound in "sing" by doubling the "i" ("siing").

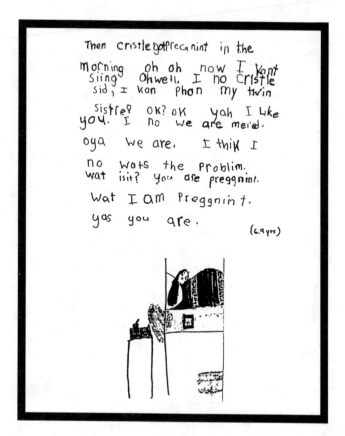

Then cristle got precinint in the
morning oh oh now I kant
siing. Ohwell. I no cristle
sid, I kan phon my twin

sistrep ok? ok yah I like
you. I no we are mered.

oya we are. I thik I

no wats the problim.
wat isit? you are preggnint.

Wat I am Preggnint.

yas you are.

(6.9yrs)

(6.9 years)

- Selection is an excerpt from one chapter of a lengthy soap opera.
- Dialogue is featured, although not marked with quotations.
- A variety of punctuation is appropriately, although not consistently, used ("OK?").
- Child's language uninhibited by lack of knowledge of "correct" way to spell words ("Wat I am preggnint").

June 11, 87. My birthday is
on the 18 of June.
On Wednesday I We
nt to mcDonalds
for a treet I Wen
t on a slide and
my sister did to
o. It was fun!!
! ! ! !! { ! { / ! / ! ! !! ! !
(6.11 yrs)

(6.11 years)

- Awareness of hyphenation, even though incorrectly employed ("we-nt"; "wen-t").
- Almost all words now conventionally spelled; punctuation used correctly (and enthusiastically!!!!!!!!).
- Capital letters appear where appropriate (first letter of sentence; proper nouns such as "Wednesday").

> Cathy "A" Christmas Story
> One Christmas nihte wen
> all was cold and dark.
> Santa came to a worm
> and neatlie deckorated
> hows. Two little girls
> and there mother and
> father woer sleping in
> bed. Santa trid tn
> get in the chimny
> exsept he was
> to fat. Then he
> tride the window
> and he still was
> to fat. Hea tried
> every plas but he
> (7.7 years)

(7.7 years)

- Excerpt from story that is complete and well crafted.
- Language reveals influence of the books she has been exposed to ("wen all was cold and dark").
- Constructive spelling still evident ("nihte" for "night"; "woer" for "were") where needed.
- Child is clearly aware of the range of possible options for representing different sounds, if yet unsure which is conventionally correct ("trid," "tride," and "tried").

How The Skunk Got His Stripe
Cathy   Nov. 24

Once there was a skunk that lived long ago. It was all black, but one day he went to a paint factory. He was just minding his own bisnuss sunnly a mon with a paintbrush swung his paint brush with paint on it on the poor little skunk. Then he ran home to tell everyone what happend then went home. He thought that it looked nice with it on but he went to have a bath in the pond and it didn't come off. But when he went outside all of the skunks were gone. There was a note on a stump and it read: To skunk we have gone to the paint factory from: THE Gang. An hour later they came home all with a stripe on it's back. They all had a BIG smile on their faces.

8.4 yrs,

(8.4 years)

- Uppercase letters now used deliberately to heighten impact ("a BIG smile").
- Colon used effectively.
- Child has made a "good copy" of her story and now has the fine motor control, and perhaps patience, to print neatly, controlling size and placement of the letters on the lines (contrast with sample produced at 7.7 years).

Blank Form for
First-Day Name Book

◆

What's in a Name?

Learning one's own name, in written form, is a milestone event. The child's name is almost invariably the first written word learned. Usually, the initial letter is recognized and written first. Gradually, the other letters are learned, although sometimes their order is mixed and some are left out. By the time a child can write his name, he has already learned a lot about how written language works. He knows that particular letters in a particular order represent his name, and that the relationship between sound and symbol is not random. Being able to write his name and the names of family members, friends and classmates can be the entry point for learning how to write. It's an accomplishment that merits recognition.

This book was written by

————————————————

Age _____

September ____, 19__

Teacher: The children can draw a picture and record their name and any other writing they wish to do. This becomes a record of the work done at the start of the year.

Parent: With your child you might like to record a highlight of his/her first day at school.

Shared Goal Setting Form

• ◆ •

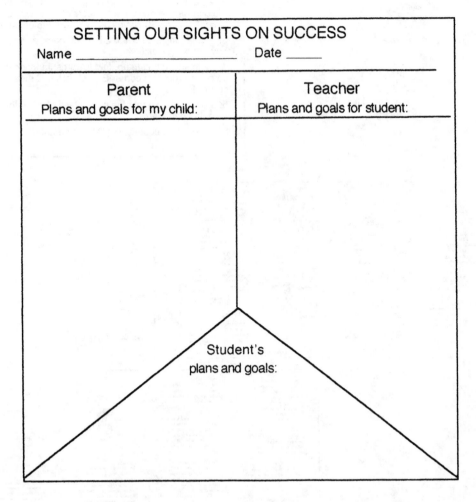

SETTING OUR SIGHTS ON SUCCESS

Name _____   Date _____

Parent	Teacher
Plans and goals for my child:	Plans and goals for student:

Student's
plans and goals:

◆

Putting the Handout (Figure 5-5) Together

Putting the Handout Together

1. Duplicate Figure 5.5 (pages 60-64).

2. Arrange handout pamphlet pages as indicated in the diagram below, on two sheets of legal size paper. Note that page 60 copies as two separate columns.

3. Photocopy side 1 and 2 back-to-back, so you have one legal size sheet.

4. With side 2 facing up, fold towards the middle so corner A meets corner B, and corner C meets corner B.

5. Fold again, so that the pamphlet looks like the sample on the left.

6. Make extra copies, they'll be in demand!

← Side 1

Side 2 →

Spring
Newspaper

Spring Newspaper

I have frens that like to Rite about cats. and so Do I. It is fun Bkos cats are Nis. I gast get inchrasted in Riting aBout cats.

Theo

We hv hyacnths in a clas. ps my mom gv thm to as.

Philip

My clds room went for a Woc to lok at SiNs We So a Stop Sin and a cros Wok Sin.

Brooke

We are eggs hatching

We hav in eore a copooder in oure clas room. we like it. It is nis.

Ryan

I braing a bees nest to school

Jennifer

Class News

One day a little robn was flying aroon and got hrt

thanthe S.P.C.A came andtoke hem away.

Kimberly

I like Dinosors Dinosors Dinosors. I like Dinosors. Blak wons and pik wons to the end

Andrew

Megan is going to DSte land. Lasa is going to Jog J.

Katrina

We are planting pole beens in are cladesroom and we made a grafe, the plantse getting

bigen eech weec and month.

Yojo

I like playing basktboll. It is fun. Smtls I git basklts.

Michael D.

H.O.cey.
We Pla Hocey
in The Jim

Mike

Sports

My fernds and me play tennis at school. We go home and haf a snak. Then we go bak to the school to play some mre tennis.

Three wecs a go The grap sevengs gTLs wr Doing Jaz dase en the Jem and The hot Scool wes wo ching The wr Juming and spe ne hing and moving Ther Legs and smleting and smiling.

Sloni

Weather Report

weather
Noo to the veather rept wth Philip Splle sune pee Tues. cloud Rain d snow

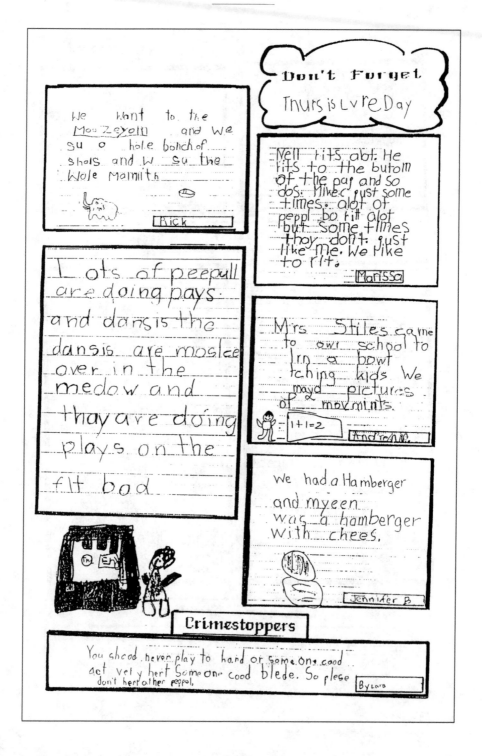

Don't Forget

Thurs is Lvre Day

We want to the Moszeyoui and we su o hole bonch of shals and w su the Wole Mamilth

Rick

Nell tits abt. He tits to the butom of the pag and so dos. Mikec just some times. alot of peppl bo tit alot but some times thay don't just like me. We like to rlt.

Marissa

Lots of peepull are doing pays and dansis the dansis are moslee over in the medow and thay are doing plays on the flt bod

Mrs Stiles came to owr school to lrn a bowt tching kids We mayd pictures of movmints.

$1+1=2$

Andrenie

We had a Hamberger and myeen was a hamberger with chees.

Jennifer B

Crimestoppers

You shood never play to hard or some one cood act vel y hert Some one cood blede. So plese don't hert other peppol.

By Lara

Resource Books for Teachers That We Particulary Recommend

◆

Bissex, G.L. 1980. GNYS *at* WRK. Cambridge, MA: Harvard University Press.
A classic longitudinal case study of one child's growth as a reader and writer between the ages of five and eleven. Bissex documents how Paul, her son, constructs his understanding of the range, functions, and mechanisms of written language, and in so doing, deepens our understanding of invented spelling.

Newman, J. 1984. *The Craft of Children's Writing.* Portsmouth, NH: Heinemann.
Newman's book is concise, reader-friendly, and genuinely informative. Using judiciously selected examples and case studies, she analyzes children's writing in terms of *"intention, organization, experimentation, and orchestration"* (p.5).

Tarasoff, M. 1992. A *Guide to Children's Spelling Development for Parents & Teachers.* Victoria, B.C.: Active Learning Institute.
Clearly written, and generously illustrated with examples taken from children's writing, this book explains how children develop spelling skills and strategies and suggests how adults can help them become aware of spelling patterns and complexities. Specific and detailed information about common spelling patterns is provided, and time spent this way will ultimately support writing development.

Wilde, S. 1992. *You Kan Red This! Spelling and Punctuation for Whole Language*, K-6. Portsmouth, NH: Heinemann.

An excellent, easy-to-read, and thoroughly researched resource for the teacher. Wilde provides a richly detailed account of the nature and complexities of spelling and illustrates the "predictable developmental paths that young spellers and users of punctuation follow" with illuminating samples of children's writing. The bulk of the book is devoted to classroom practice and is designed to help teachers support children's learning of the conventions of written language. Peppered with practical ideas, strategies, sound guidelines, and instructive anecdotes, the book will prove a valuable and welcome resource.

Glossary

◆

These are terms you will find parents are not always clear about.

Integrated literacy approach

This is a "philosophical stance" (Newman, 1985, p. 1) regarding a curriculum rich in language and literature with the possibility that both areas be fully integrated across the various subject disciplines. Instruction does not rely on a single basal series and the use of worksheets. The teacher's responsibility is to set up an environment in which the child is encouraged to initiate and generate ideas and to actively engage in a broad range of reading and writing experiences. Skills are taught in context, ideally when the child indicates an interest in them or a need for them. The learner takes responsibility for his or her learning within an ever-expanding, challenging, and supportive environment. The approach takes into consideration the individual nature, interests, and background of each learner. The aim is to facilitate learning that is personally purposeful, meaningful, and enjoyable, while enabling the child to progress at his/her own pace. Such a curriculum values the importance of informed parents.

Whole language

This term frequently is used to refer to what has just been described above as an integrated literacy approach. Vacca and Rasinski (1992) describe whole language as a philosophy, or "professional theory of education," which recognizes language and meaning making as intertwined, and language learning as inherently social. "Keeping language 'whole' means not breaking it into bits and pieces or isolating the subsystems of language for instructional emphasis" (p. 7). It means understanding that language is learned from whole to part, and not the other way around. Whole-language theorists believe children learn written language in much the same way they learned to speak—"naturally and informally." As a result, they advocate the immersion of children in print-rich, literate classroom environments and their engagement in genuine and varied communication situations that have point and purpose evident to the learner.

Emergent writer

"Emergent" is a term used to refer to learners who are just beginning to explore and understand the functions and complexities of our writing system. Harste, Woodward, and Burke (1984) caution that the term implies a maturationist view of literacy that erroneously underplays the critical role of the child's experience. "Emergent" is an attempt to convey the sense of naturalness and growth. However, the active role of the learner in directing and driving development needs to be stressed. Becoming a writer is neither a passive unfolding nor a developmental inevitability.

The writing process

The phrase attempts to describe the various processes and strategies writers engage in and employ when they write. "Theorists describe the writing process in different ways: as pre-writing, writing, and re-writing; as circling out and circling back; as collecting and connecting. . . . [as] rehearsal, drafting, revision, and editing" (Calkins, 1986, p. 17). The activity of writing is dynamic and recursive, not linear; the constituent processes typically occur simultaneously and interactively.

Constructive/functional/invented spellings

These terms refer to the logical, if unconventional, spellings used by children while they are working out the rules that govern conventional or standard spelling. Read (1975) describes these "inventions" as indicators of a "spelling system" that a young writer constructs to express his language based on the speech sounds and a partial knowledge of letter names and standard spelling. Far from being, as initially thought, simply a stage on the way to conventional spelling, it is instead a strategy used by spellers of all ages when attempting to produce unfamiliar words.

Convention

Conventions can be thought of as social rules, intended to facilitate communication, that govern language use and form. Convention refers to the socially accepted, expected, and "correct" ways of doing things.

Standard or conventional spellings

Conventional spellings are understood to be those that are found in the dictionary and generally accepted as "correct."

Readable

"Readable" describes written work that can easily be deciphered regardless of how standard the spelling is.

References

Ahlberg, J. & A. 1986. *The Jolly Postman, or Other People's Letters*. London: Heinemann.

Anthony, R., Johnson, T., Mickelson, N., & Preece, A. 1991. *Evaluating Literacy: A Perspective for Change*. Portsmouth, NH: Heinemann.

Baskwill, J. 1989. *Parents and Teachers—Partners in Learning*. Richmond Hill, Ont: Scholastic-Tab Publications.

British Columbia Ministry of Education. 1991. *Supporting Learning; A Resource for Parents and Teachers*.

Calkins, L. 1990. *Living Between the Lines*. Portsmouth, NH: Heinemann.

Calkins, L. 1986. *The Art of Teaching Writing*. Portsmouth, NH: Heinemann.

Clark, D., Lotto, S., & MacCarthy, M. 1980. "Factors Associated with Success in Urban Elementary Schools." *Phi Delta Kappan*, 61(7): 467–70.

Doake, D. 1988, *Reading Begins at Birth*, Richmond Hill, Ont: Scholastic-Tab Publications.

Epstein, J.L. 1988. "Effects on Student Achievement of Teachers' Practices for Parent Involvement." In S. Silvern (Ed.), *Literacy through Family, Community, and School Interaction*. Greenwich, CT: JAI Press.

Epstein, J.L. 1986. "Parents' Reactions to Teacher Practices of Parent Involvement." *Elementary School Journal*, 86(3): 277–94.

Fields, M. 1988. "Talking and Writing: Explaining the Whole Language Approach to Parents." *The Reading Teacher*, May: p. 902.

Fields, M.V. 1989. *Literacy begins at birth*. Tucson, Arizona: Fisher Books

Forester, A., Reinhard, M. 1989. *The Learner's Way*. Winnipeg, Man.: Peguis.

Fullan, M. G., with Stiegelbauer, S. 1991. *The New Meaning of Educational Change* (2nd ed.). New York: Teachers College Press.

Gentry, J.R. 1987. *Spel . . . Is a Four-Letter Word*. Portsmouth, NH: Heinemann.

Graves, D. 1983. *Writing: Teachers and Children at Work*. Portsmouth, NH: Heinemann.

Graves D., & Stuart, V. 1985. *Write from the Start*. New York: New American Library.

Gunderson, L., & Shapiro, J. 1988. "Whole Language Instruction: Writing in First Grade." *The Reading Teacher*, 41(4): p. 430–37

Harste, J., Woodward, V., & Burke, C. 1984. *Language Stories and Literacy Lessons*. Portsmouth, NH: Heinemann.

James, D. 1989. "Parent Involvement." *Research Forum*, 5, Fall.

Katz, L.G. 1991. Cited in *Supporting Learning: A Resource for Parents and Teachers*. British Columbia Ministry of Education, p. 17

Kraus, R. 1971. *Leo the Late Bloomer*. New York: Windmill Books.

Kress, G. 1982. *Learning to Write*. London: Routledge & Kegan Paul.

Mickelson, N.I. 1990. Plenary Address. The Whole Language Institute. University of Victoria, B.C. Canada.

Newman, J. (Ed.). 1985. *Whole Language: Theory in Use*. Portsmouth, NH: Heinemann.

Read, C. 1975. *Children's Categorization of Speech Sounds in English*. Urbana, Illinois: NCTE .

Reinhard, M. 1989. Personal communication.

Rich, D. 1988. *Megaskills: How Families Can Help Children Succeed in School and Beyond*. Boston, MA: Houghton Mifflin.

Routman, R. 1988. *Transitions: From Literature to Literacy*. Portsmouth, NH: Heinemann.

Smith, F. 1982. *Writing and the Writer*. New York: Holt, Rinehart & Winston.
Smith, F. 1986. *Insult to Intelligence*. New York: Arbor House.

Tarasoff, M. 1992. *A Guide to Children's Spelling Development for Parents and Teachers*. Victoria, B.C.: Active Learning Institute.

Vacca, R.T., & Rasinski, T.V. 1992. *Case Studies in Whole Language*. New York: Harcourt Brace Jovanovich College Publishers.
Villiers, U. 1989. LUK MUME LUK DADE I KAN RIT. Richmond Hill, Ont., Canada: Scholastic-TAB.

Wells, G. 1981. "Language and Learning". Address given at Conference on Language Development, Parksville B.C.

Yates, T., and Ryan, D. 1987. *Young Writers at Work*. NSW: Methuen.
Young, E. 1992. *Seven Blind Mice*. New York: Philomel Books.

Index